# SELF-CARE FOR TEACHERS

## OPTIMIZE YOUR PERFORMANCE, ACHIEVE FULFILLMENT, AND REVITALIZE THE JOYS OF TEACHING WITHOUT COMPROMISING WORK-LIFE BALANCE

## LEARN AND TEACH HUB

*To my beloved Clement, the pillar of my life and the rock of our family, this dedication is a testament to the love and admiration I hold for you. Your unwavering support and devotion have been a guiding light through every joy and challenge we've faced together.*

*To my cherished stepdaughter Annamarie, you are a precious gift that blended seamlessly into our lives. Your presence brings so much joy and love, and I'm grateful for the bond we share as a family.*

*To my dear son Robin, your kind heart and boundless ambition inspire me every day. Watching you grow and succeed fills my heart with pride and love beyond measure.*

*To my precious son Ramon, your warm smile and gentle soul light up our lives. Your journey through life is a source of immense happiness for us, and I'm forever thankful to call you, my son.*

*To my wonderful daughter-in-law Maila, your love and care for our family are deeply appreciated. You have enriched our lives with your presence, and I'm thankful for the happiness you bring to my son's life.*

*To my adorable grandson Silas, you are the future and a ray of hope. Your laughter and innocence bring so much joy to our hearts, and I cherish every moment we spend together.*

*To my loving sisters, your unwavering support and camaraderie have been a source of strength throughout our lives. Together, we've shared laughter, tears, and unforgettable memories, making our bond unbreakable.*

*To my dear dad Max, your guidance, love, and sacrifices have shaped me into the person I am today. You have been my rock, and I will forever carry your wisdom and affection in my heart.*

*To my mom in heaven, though you are no longer with us in the physical realm, your spirit and love remain alive in our hearts. Your memory continues to inspire and guide me, and I find comfort in knowing you watch over us from above.*

*This dedication is a tribute to the remarkable people in my life who have filled it with love, laughter, and endless support. Together, you form the foundation of my happiness, and I am truly blessed to have each of you in my life.*

# FOREWORD

I come from a lineage of educators. On my mother's side, both of my grandparents were teachers, and one of my mother's sisters pursued teaching as a profession. Even my own mother taught me math during my first year of high school. On my father's side, two of my aunts were also teachers. It's no surprise that growing up, I aspired to become a teacher myself.

My sisters and I resided with our grandparents on an island, alongside our cousins from my mother's side. Our house was situated by the beach, and we would spend our weekends and summer vacations swimming all day long. We would only return home to have lunch and then rush back to the water until it got dark.

When I was in the fourth grade, a school rented a room on the ground floor of my grandparents' house to use as a classroom. One beautiful summer day, I bought some candies and proposed to my sisters and cousins that I would reward them during break time if they played the roles of students while I acted as their teacher. They eagerly agreed, and at that moment, my dream of becoming a teacher unexpectedly came true. They listened attentively and actively participated in the "class." However, when the promised break time arrived, I instructed my students to return after 15 minutes before distributing the candies. And what happened next? You guessed it right. They never came back; instead, they spent the rest of the day swimming.

When the time came for me to attend college, my relatives advised me against pursuing education as a major. They warned that becoming a grade schoolteacher would likely lead to spinsterhood. My parents suggested studying accounting instead, with the option to teach college students if I still desired to teach after graduation. I heeded their advice, obtained a degree in accounting, got married, had two children, worked as an accountant, and tragically became a widow at the age of 29. Yet, my passion for teaching never waned.

In 2010, inspired by the memory of my mother who passed away in 2008, I started serving at church. I had never officially volunteered, but when asked, I couldn't bring myself to refuse. A few days after our new church was inaugurated, I went to visit and prayed for my lottery ticket, which I had brought with me, to win. While I was there, immersed in prayer, the members of the Lector ministry were recording themselves while reading and providing feedback to one another. The coordinator spotted me and invited me to step up to the microphone and read. Though hesitant, I eventually acquiesced to her persistent request. Before long, she asked me to join their group, and being someone who struggles to say no, I accepted.

During my three years as a lector, I got to know individuals from other ministries within the church. In 2013, while assisting in serving snacks to the CFF (Christian Formation for Children) teachers during their yearly meeting, one of the teachers asked if I would volunteer to teach fourth grade. Without hesitation, I agreed.

I didn't possess a degree in education, nor had I received any formal training. In my first year of teaching, we were invited to a retreat where we received some teaching tips, along with the teacher guide, textbooks, and workbooks for our students. However, on the very first day of that school year, I found myself unsure of how to begin the class. Balancing a full-time job, I had limited time to create lesson plans, so I simply instructed my students to follow the directions in their workbooks. I had no understanding that each student learns differently, and the only teaching method I knew was lecturing. Consequently, my students grew bored, became disruptive, and made a lot of noise. After that incident, I was tempted to quit, but our Parish needed help as there were few volunteers available. So, despite the challenges, I chose to stay and continue teaching.

Among the volunteer teachers in our Church, some were professionals in the field. They generously conducted workshops for us during our annual kick-off meetings. As time passed, I discovered valuable tools for lesson planning and effective classroom management.

In November 2022, I unfortunately suffered injuries, breaking five ribs and my right clavicle. This compelled me to take a break from teaching and provided an opportunity for deep reflection on my teaching journey. I asked myself critical questions: Did my students truly learn and grow under my guidance? Why did I encounter struggles in my initial year of teaching? Was I the only one facing these difficulties? What could I have done differently to enhance their learning experience? Why did I contemplate quitting at certain points? Moreover, I pondered over the scarcity of volunteers and the reasons behind their departure.

Driven by these inquiries, I embarked on thorough research to identify the common reasons for teacher attrition. I delved into understanding what factors contribute to their happiness and commitment to the profession. I sought to learn more about both teachers and their students, recognizing that learning capacities vary across age groups and that there exist four types of learning styles. I discovered concepts like the "52 17 rule," the Pomodoro Technique, and the importance of primal break time. I also explored practical methods for preparing engaging lesson plans, incorporating age-appropriate exercises, employing attention-grabbing techniques, and utilizing effective assessment tools.

The culmination of this journey led me to write a book centered around teacher self-care. It aims to support educators in achieving a healthy work-life balance while enabling them to thrive as exceptional teachers.

# CONTENTS

# INTRODUCTION

Welcome, dear reader, to this metamorphic journey. I am thrilled that you've chosen to embark on this voyage with me as we explore the path to rediscovering joy and purpose in your teaching career.

Teaching is not merely a profession but a calling that reaches deep into the souls of those who hear its whisper. It is an act of unwavering dedication, a commitment to guiding young minds, and an unwavering belief in the potential of each student who enters your classroom. As educators, we possess an incredible power—the power to change lives, inspire dreams, and ignite the flames of knowledge.

In the hearts of our students, we become heroes. We become the mentors, role models, and guiding lights illuminating their path toward a brighter future. We have the privilege of witnessing the transformation of young minds as they grow, learn, and realize their full potential. And in those moments, we stand tall, knowing that we have played an irreplaceable part in shaping the world.

However, dear reader, with great power comes great responsibility. As educators, if we do not prioritize our own well-being and practice self-care, we risk becoming the villains in our own stories. The burden of our responsibilities can overwhelm us, leading to physical, emotional, and mental exhaustion. The passion that once fueled us can flicker and dim, leaving us drained and disconnected.

Yet, let us not dwell on the darkness. Instead, let us focus on the light within us—the flame of enthusiasm, the fuel of inspiration, and the source of our power to change the world.

This esteemed profession's challenges are not in short supply. Research shows that teacher burnout is prevalent, and the job demands can affect physical, emotional, and mental well-being. Perhaps you find yourself questioning what led you to this point. How did a profession filled with so much passion and promise become overshadowed by stress, exhaustion, and a sense of being overwhelmed?

I empathize with your pain because I've been there too. As a volunteer teacher, I have experienced the highs and lows of this noble profession firsthand. I have observed the dedication and tireless efforts of educators like you, who go above and beyond to make a difference in the lives of their students. And it is precisely because of this shared understanding that I am here to support you on this journey toward self-care and personal growth.

What brought you to this book? What catalyst propelled you to seek guidance and support? It might be the lingering exhaustion that seeps into every aspect of your life or the feeling of losing touch with the joys that drew you to teaching in the first place. No matter your motive, rest assured that you are not alone.

Throughout the upcoming pages, we will embark on a transformative process together. This book is designed to be your compass, guiding you toward a renewed sense of purpose, fulfillment, and work-life balance. It is packed with practical strategies, real-life anecdotes, and research-backed insights to help you navigate your unique challenges as a teacher.

Armed with the Le.AR.N. Method—Let go, Accept & Realign, and Nurture—we will unlock the secrets to sustainable self-care and holistic well-being. This framework acknowledges that every teacher's journey is unique and provides a flexible roadmap tailored to your needs and lifestyle.

Throughout our exploration, we will challenge self-limiting beliefs, perfectionism, and the need for control. We will learn to accept help, realign our priorities and goals, and nurture our health, relationships, and inner world, rekindling the passions and hobbies that bring us joy.

Nevertheless, don't solely rely on my word for it. This method has transformed the lives of countless educators who have found renewed purpose, balance, and joy in their profession. Now, it's your chance to encounter the profound transformation that awaits you.

Imagine a life where you wake up excited to go to work, where stress and burnout are distant memories. Picture yourself confidently navigating the classroom challenges with a toolkit of strategies that engage and inspire your students. Envision a future where you prioritize your health, nurture meaningful relationships, and have the energy and enthusiasm to pursue your personal goals.

It is a tremendous honor to be guided on this journey. Together, we will create a roadmap to reclaim the joys of teaching and cultivate a thriving, balanced life. So, take a deep breath, dear reader, and know you have made the right choice. The path to self-care and fulfillment begins now.

# 1

## WHAT'S HOLDING YOU BACK?

Now, let us pause for a moment and revisit the inception of your teaching journey. Do you remember the exhilarating mix of nervousness and excitement filling your heart as you entered a classroom brimming with students? The dreams you held close, the passion that fueled you, and the unwavering belief that you would make a difference in their lives. It was a time of hope, limitless possibilities, and pure joy.

Reflecting on my experience, I recall my first encounter with a class of eager minds. The room buzzed with anticipation, and I couldn't help but feel a mixture of exhilaration and a touch of trepidation. The weight of responsibility settled on me, and the desire to create a nurturing, inspiring learning environment overwhelmed me. It was a pivotal moment that shaped my path as an educator.

Let us bridge the gap between that initial excitement and the present moment. Take a moment to travel back to the inception of your teaching journey. How have you evolved since those early days? How do you feel about teaching now, compared to that sense of joy and purpose that ignited your passion in the first place?

It's crucial to take this introspective journey, for it is within us that we often find the answers to what's holding us back from experiencing the complete joy of teaching. We all have those self-limiting beliefs and behaviors that confine us within the boundaries of what we think a teacher should be. Our growth, fulfillment, and ability to thrive in the classroom can be impeded by these unseen constraints.

So, my dear friend, let us embark on a journey of self-discovery, where we unveil and release the shackles that hold us back. This chapter serves as a springboard for that journey as we explore the depths of our own perceptions, beliefs, and limitations. The goal is to gain a deeper awareness of what keeps us confined within the boxed idea of being a teacher.

It's time to ask ourselves those critical questions. What beliefs have we held onto that limit our potential? Have we succumbed to the pressures of perfectionism or the need for control? Are we allowing self-doubt to overshadow our confidence? These inquiries are not meant to elicit self-judgment but to invite introspection, to gently unravel the layers that hold us captive and prevent us from experiencing the complete joy of teaching.

## HOW DID WE GET HERE?

Let's take a moment to understand how we arrived at this point —a place where burnout has become an all-too-familiar companion in our teaching journeys. Burnout, my friend, is not just a buzzword or a passing phase. It is a natural and significant challenge that affects countless educators, jeopardizing our well-being, effectiveness, and love for teaching.

It's essential to understand its definition and the factors contributing to its development to comprehend the depths of burnout. It is a state of chronic physical and emotional exhaustion resulting from prolonged exposure to excessive stress (Maslach & Leiter, 2016). It's a feeling of being depleted, drained, and overwhelmed physically and mentally.

While a burnout episode can be a warning from our body, it can also become chronic if we don't take care of it, leading to anxiety disorders or depression. The neurology of stress and anxiety further sheds light on how burnout takes hold. As stress grips us, our brains release stress hormones like cortisol and adrenaline. These hormones prime us for "fight or flight" reactions. However, when stress becomes chronic, our bodies remain in a continuous state of heightened alertness. This continued activation of the stress response can have adverse effects on both our physical and mental health.

Identifying the signs and symptoms of burnout is vital in addressing its influence on our lives. Emotional exhaustion, cynicism, and a reduced sense of accomplishment are common manifestations (Maslach & Leiter, 2016). We may feel emotionally drained, detached, and increasingly hostile about our work. The passion that once fueled us feels distant, overshadowed by a sense of futility and disconnection.

It is essential to recognize that burnout doesn't occur suddenly or overnight. It occurs in stages, gradually intensifying over time. The early stages may involve fatigue, irritability, and decreased motivation. We may find ourselves pushing through exhaustion, thinking it's a temporary hurdle. However, if left unaddressed, burnout progresses, manifesting in physical symptoms like headaches, sleep disturbances, and weakened immune function (Schaufeli et al., 2017). We aim to learn how to recognize these stages to intervene before burnout takes a firm grip on our lives.

But what are its causes? While internal factors like perfectionism and high self-expectations play a role, it's crucial to acknowledge the external causes that contribute to our struggles. Heavy workloads, lack of control, insufficient support, and challenging interpersonal dynamics are common culprits (Hakanen et al., 2014). The teaching profession can present overwhelming demands. When coupled with external pressures, it creates a perfect storm that propels us further into burnout.

Reflecting on my teaching career, I experienced the stages of burnout gradually but relentlessly. It began with moments of exhaustion and frustration, which I dismissed as mere side effects of the demanding profession we had chosen. Over time, those moments grew more frequent, subtly eroding my enthusiasm and zest for teaching.

I was caught in a cycle of excessive workloads, relentless self-imposed pressure, and a lack of boundaries. The signs were present, like soft whispers of caution, but I failed to give them the attention they warranted. As burnout progressively tightened its hold, I became aware of its impact on my physical, emotional, and mental well-being. It was a wake-up call—a call to reassess, seek support, and embark on a journey of self-care and renewal.

The chapters will dig deeper into strategies and techniques to address burnout head-on. Together, we will reclaim our joy, restore our well-being, and revitalize our passion for teaching.

## A LOOK WITHIN

It is time to explore the internal landscape of teachers—our thoughts, beliefs, and behaviors that shape our experiences in the classroom and beyond. In the depths of our being lie the roots of both our potential and limitations. So, let us look into the realm of limiting beliefs and uncover the power that lies within us.

Limiting beliefs are the subtle whispers of self-doubt that permeate our minds, constraining our potential and hindering our growth. As educators, we may encounter various self-limiting beliefs that restrict our progress and impede our joy in teaching. These beliefs can stem from many sources, such as societal expectations, past experiences, and comparisons to others.

Imagine, for a moment, a teacher in their first year of teaching. They may believe that to earn the trust and respect of their colleagues, administrators, and students, they must tirelessly work extra hours, go above and beyond, and sacrifice their own well-being. This belief may emerge from a desire to prove themselves worthy and capable, driven by the notion that exceeding expectations is the key to success.

These limiting beliefs manifest in various forms, each uniquely impacting our lives as educators. Some teachers may feel the need to completely control every aspect of their classroom, fearing that relinquishing management will lead to chaos or failure. Others may battle feelings of inadequacy, constantly doubting their abilities and fearing that they are not qualified or competent enough to make a significant impact.

But how do these seemingly harmless beliefs affect us in the long run? Initially, they may motivate us to work harder, strive for perfection, and demonstrate our dedication to our students. Yet, as time goes on, the weight of these beliefs can wear us down. We may neglect our well-being, sacrifice our personal lives, and ultimately succumb to burnout and exhaustion. Our mental and emotional well-being declines and our capacity to effectively connect with and support our students diminishes.

Returning to my journey, I realized that while I cannot control everything that happens to me, I can control my responses and the beliefs I choose to embrace. It was a moment of profound awakening, understanding that the path to fulfillment and success lies in shifting our perspective and nurturing an empowerment mindset.

As we embark on this journey of self-discovery, it is essential to recognize that the process is deeply personal. Each of us carries our own set of beliefs and experiences that shape our perceptions. What may limit one person may not necessarily limit another. Hence, self-reflection and introspection to recognize the self-limiting beliefs that impede our progress.

In the following chapters, we will delve into practical strategies and techniques aimed at challenging and overcoming these limiting beliefs. We will engage in reflective exercises, engage in empowering conversations, and draw upon the wisdom of historical figures and contemporary educators who have transcended their limitations. Collectively, we will initiate a transformative journey, aiming for a teaching experience that is more fulfilling and balanced.

Let us confront our limiting beliefs, redefine our narratives, and unlock our true potential as educators. The path may not always be easy, but with courage, self-compassion, and a commitment to growth, we will transcend our limitations and create a teaching experience that is joyful, impactful, and aligned with our true selves.

## WHERE DO WE GO FROM HERE?

Now that we have gained a deeper understanding of limiting beliefs and their impact on our lives as educators, it's time to chart a path toward overcoming these barriers and unlocking our true potential. This section will explore practical steps and actionable tips to identify and overcome limiting beliefs, paving the way for personal and professional growth.

To begin our journey of self-discovery, let us first explore how to identify our limiting beliefs. Recognizing these deeply ingrained patterns of thought is crucial for dismantling their hold on us and creating space for positive transformation. Fortunately, there are effective strategies we can employ to uncover and confront these beliefs head-on.

The initial step to overcoming limiting beliefs is to develop an awareness of them. It is crucial to recognize and comprehend the thoughts and ideas that might hinder you from reaching your full potential as a teacher. To do this, let's walk through a series of steps to help you identify and shed light on your limiting beliefs.

Take a moment to reflect on your inner thoughts and beliefs about yourself, your abilities, and your role as an educator. What recurring patterns or narratives emerge? Are there any self-doubts, fears, or beliefs limiting your growth? For example, you might think I need to be better at handling challenging students, or I can't balance my personal life and teaching responsibilities.

Let me share a personal anecdote illustrating how you can navigate this process. When I started my teaching career, I needed to work on my ability to engage students effectively. I needed to be more creative and charismatic to connect with them. However, reflecting on these thoughts and beliefs, I realized that they were merely self-imposed limitations stemming from my insecurities and comparing myself to others. This self-awareness was pivotal in my journey toward overcoming my limiting beliefs.

After identifying your limiting beliefs, the next step is to take action and conquer them. Allow me to provide you with practical tips that will empower you to challenge and transform your beliefs:

- **Question the validity of your beliefs:** Take a critical look at your limiting beliefs and ask yourself whether they are based on actual evidence or simply self-imposed perceptions. Challenge the assumptions and negative narratives that underpin these beliefs. Let's say you believe that you must work extra hours and sacrifice your well-being to be considered a dedicated teacher. Challenge this belief by considering alternative ways to demonstrate dedication and effectiveness, such as prioritizing self-care and setting boundaries.

- **Substitute negative self-talk affirmations:** Replace self-limiting thoughts with positive statements that counteract those beliefs. Affirmations are powerful tools for reprogramming your mind and fostering a positive mindset. Repeat statements like, I am capable of growth and success as an educator, or I embrace challenges as opportunities for growth. Whenever you think I'm not good enough, replace it with, I am constantly growing and improving in my teaching practice.

- **Look for support and encouragement**: Build a nurturing circle of colleagues, mentors, or fellow educators who can provide guidance, motivation, and a new outlook on things. Share your challenges and aspirations with them, drawing strength from their support. Give thought to finding a mentor or becoming part of a professional learning community where you can exchange experiences, learn from others, and receive support during difficult moments.

- **Set small, achievable goals**: Break your larger goals into smaller, manageable steps. Setting achievable goals creates a sense of progress and accomplishment, which helps to counteract self-doubt and reinforce a growth mindset. If you feel overwhelmed by incorporating technology into your teaching, start with a specific goal, such as learning to use one new educational app or platform.

- **Welcome failure as a chance to learn**: Recognize that setbacks and failures are inherent aspects of the learning journey. Embrace them as opportunities for growth and reflection rather than viewing them as indicators of your worth or competence as a teacher. If a lesson doesn't go as planned, take the time to reflect on what didn't work and what you can learn from the experience to improve your future teaching practices.

- **Cultivate self-compassion**: Show kindness to yourself throughout as you navigate the journey of overcoming limiting beliefs. Extend to yourself the same compassion and understanding you would offer to a dear friend. Acknowledge and celebrate your progress, regardless of how small it may seem, and practice patience with yourself during challenging moments. When you make a mistake, remind yourself that it is part of the learning process and an opportunity for growth. Treat yourself with kindness and forgiveness. It's important to remember that beliefs are not formed overnight. They result from our experiences, conditioning, and interpretations of the world. Escaping the grip of limiting beliefs can prove challenging, as they have become deeply ingrained within our being. However, we can gradually transform these beliefs with self-reflection, self-compassion, and a commitment to growth. Growth is not a linear journey. Recognize that progress may not always be a straightforward path, and there will be both ups and downs along the way. A bad day or setback does not mean you have failed entirely. Each day is an opportunity for growth and learning from your experiences.

## What's Holding You Back?

| Questions | Sample Answer | Your Answer |
| --- | --- | --- |
| How did you feel during the initial days of your teaching journey? | A mix of nervousness and excitement. | |
| What were the dreams and convictions that fueled your passion for teaching at the beginning? | The excitement of being responsible for shaping young minds. | |
| How has your perception changed since the early days of teaching? | Better understanding of how to help students as opposed to simply having the eagerness to do so. | |
| Why is self-reflection important for gaining a deeper awareness of your role as a teacher? | Self-reflection helps in understanding the role of a teacher. | |
| How can exploring personal growth contribute to a more fulfilling teaching experience? | Exploring personal growth is significant when trying to enhance a teacher's skills. | |
| Have you experienced any of the signs of burnout mentioned in the chapter, such as emotional exhaustion or detachment? | Yes, but that's a common sentiment among teachers that disappears once they find purpose in their roles. | |
| Reflect on a time when you felt detached or hostile about your work, and how it impacted your teaching? | Frustration is often part of the job, and it did impact my eagerness to teach, but the reasons for it have little to do with the job itself. | |
| How did burnout manifest in your teaching journey, and what were the early signs you may have overlooked? | Lack of confidence in my teacher's skills and less enthusiasm about the job. | |

| | | |
|---|---|---|
| **Explore the internal and external causes of burnout in your teaching experience.** | There are many factors, such as excessive workloads, and self-imposed pressure. | |
| **How did you reassess, seek support, and embark on a journey of self-care to counter burnout?** | It's always good to try and remember why you became a teacher in the first place and also remember that everybody has bad days, even if they have nothing to do with the job. | |
| **Identify a current limiting belief about your teaching abilities.** | The lack of progress with some students. | |
| **In what ways do these limiting beliefs impact your overall well-being and effectiveness as a teacher?** | Increase of stress and impact on confidence levels. | |
| **From where do these limiting beliefs originate, considering past experiences, societal expectations, or comparisons with others?** | Comparison to others in the same job role, or past experiences. | |
| **How has challenging the validity of your beliefs positively influenced your teaching practice?** | By setting boundaries and prioritizing self-care, which improved my effectiveness as a teacher. | |
| **Share your experience of embracing failure as a learning opportunity in your teaching journey.** | Embracing failure means embracing a growth mindset and viewing setbacks as opportunities to grow. | |
| **Why are self-compassion and patience crucial in self-awareness and introspection, and how do you practice them?** | Understanding shortcomings without criticizing yourself helps create objective exploration of feelings and thoughts. | |

# 2

# WHAT'S STRESSING YOU OUT?

In this chapter, we will explore the various stressors that teachers face and look into the impact these stressors can have on their well-being.

To effectively address the stressors that teachers face, it is essential to have a solid understanding of what stress is and how it impacts our lives, so let's start by defining what it is.

Stress is the body's natural response to any demand or challenge that requires adaptation or adjustment (Cleveland Clinic, n.d.). This is the body's method of preparing for potential threats or perceived dangers. While moderate levels of stress can be beneficial in certain situations, chronic or excessive stress can negatively impact our physical and mental well-being. It can present itself in diverse ways, and its symptoms can differ from one person to another. Typical symptoms of stress encompass headaches, muscle tension, fatigue, changes in appetite, and sleep disturbances. Emotionally, stress may lead to irritability, mood swings, anxiety, and difficulties with concentration. It can also lead to behavioral changes, such as increased reliance on unhealthy coping mechanisms like excessive eating, alcohol consumption, or withdrawal from social activities.

The causes of stress are varied and highly individualized. The same stressor can impact individuals differently; what causes stress for one person might not have the same effect on another. It's essential to recognize that everyone's perception and response to stressors can differ. As teachers, you may encounter specific stressors related to your profession. Some of them may include:

- **Workload and time pressure:** Balancing lesson planning, grading, administrative tasks, and classroom management can create significant time constraints and increased work demands.
- **Student behavior and discipline issues:** Challenging student behavior and the need to address discipline issues can add to the stress teachers experience.
- **High expectations and accountability:** Teachers often face pressure to meet performance standards and achieve desired educational outcomes, creating feelings of pressure and stress.
- **Limited resources and support:** Insufficient resources, lack of support, and a perceived lack of control over decision-making can contribute to stress levels.

- **Work-life balance:** Teachers often experience significant stress while juggling personal responsibilities, family commitments, and striving for a healthy work-life.

Does everyone experience stress? Yes, it is a universal human experience and an evolutive biological response. While the specific stressors may differ, virtually everyone encounters some stress.

Inadequately managing stress can result in mental and physical health problems. Persistent stress can compromise the immune system, elevate the likelihood of developing chronic conditions like heart disease, and have adverse effects on mental health, contributing to anxiety, depression, and burnout. Additionally, unmanaged stress can impair cognitive functioning, decision-making abilities, and interpersonal relationships. Recognizing the significance of actively coping with and managing stress is crucial to prevent these unfavorable consequences.

Teachers today are experiencing heightened stress levels, particularly in light of recent disruptions in the education system. Research from the RAND Corporation reveals that teachers and principals report frequent job-related stress at twice the rate of the general working population (Steiner et al., 2022). The challenges brought about by the COVID-19 pandemic, managing student behavior, staffing shortages, low salaries, and addressing interrupted learning have become significant stressors for teachers. Furthermore, teachers of color, mid-career teachers, and female educators often experience lower levels of well-being, which can be attributed to factors such as racial discrimination and juggling work and caregiving responsibilities.

Take a moment to reflect on your own experiences and ask yourself: What are the primary stressors in my teaching role? Is it the challenge of remote learning? Managing student behavior? Staffing shortages? Low salaries? The initial step in devising strategies to address stressors is identifying and pinpointing them.

Throughout these pages, we will learn how to create a compelling and personalized plan to deal with the responses and symptoms of stress, but first, we must continue learning about its nature and how it manifests itself.

## WHAT DO YOU DO WHEN YOU'RE STRESSED?

Imagine yourself in the bustling hallways of a school, surrounded by students rushing to their classes and the weight of responsibilities resting on your shoulders. Teaching can be a gratifying profession but comes with its fair share of stress, burnout, and anxiety. As educators, we must empower ourselves with the tools to navigate these challenges and prioritize our well-being. That's why, in this chapter, we embark on a journey to explore the art of coping. By delving into various coping strategies, mechanisms, and styles, we aim to empower you with a comprehensive understanding of how to effectively manage stress in your teaching career.

Researchers have identified four categories of coping that individuals commonly employ when facing stressors (Lazarus & Folkman, 1984). These categories include problem-focused coping, emotion-focused coping, seeking social support, and avoidance coping. Let's examine each type more closely and explore relevant examples to aid in distinguishing them:

**1. Problem-focused coping:** This form of coping centers on actively addressing the underlying cause of the stressor. It entails taking concrete steps to resolve the problem and maximize its impact on your well-being. For instance, if you're feeling overwhelmed with your workload, you may employ problem-focused coping by creating a schedule, prioritizing tasks, and seeking additional resources or support to manage your responsibilities effectively.

**2. Emotion-focused coping:** This coping approach involves regulating and managing the emotions linked to the stressor. It aims to reduce emotional distress and promote emotional well-being. For example, suppose you're feeling anxious before an important presentation. In that case, you might engage in emotion-focused coping by practicing relaxation techniques, deep breathing exercises, or mindfulness meditation to calm your mind and alleviate stress.

**3. Seeking social support:** This coping category entails reaching out to others for help, guidance, and understanding. Seeking social help can provide a sense of validation, comfort, and perspective. When facing a particularly challenging situation, you may seek social support by confiding in a trusted colleague, discussing your concerns with a friend or family member, or participating in support groups or professional networks.

**4. Avoidance coping:** This refers to attempts to steer clear of or distract oneself from the stressor instead of directly confronting it. This coping style might offer temporary relief, but it does not address the root problem. Examples of avoidance coping include procrastination, excessive use of technology or substances, or engaging in activities that temporarily escape the stressor, such as binge-watching television shows or mindlessly scrolling through social media.

Coping mechanisms can also be categorized into different types based on their specific nature and purpose. Let's explore these types and provide relevant examples for each:

1. Active coping: Involves taking direct action to address the stressor or its impact. Examples of active coping include problem-solving, seeking information or guidance, and engaging in physical or mental activities that help manage stress effectively.

2. Passive coping: On the other hand, this approach involves more tolerant and less proactive strategies. It may include daydreaming, withdrawing from social interactions, or engaging in wishful thinking without taking active steps to address the stressor.

3. Adaptive coping involves employing healthy and constructive strategies to manage stress and build resilience. Adaptive coping includes regular exercise, practicing relaxation techniques, journaling, seeking therapy or counseling, and maintaining a balanced lifestyle. These coping mechanisms promote long-term well-being and help you effectively and healthily navigate stressors.

**5. Maladaptive coping** refers to using unhealthy or harmful strategies to deal with stress. These coping mechanisms may provide temporary relief but can negatively affect your well-being. Examples of maladaptive coping include excessive alcohol or drug use, emotional eating, withdrawing from social interactions, and engaging in self-destructive behaviors. Being aware of these maladaptive coping mechanisms is crucial, and it is important to strive toward replacing them with healthier alternatives.

As you will have noticed, the last strategy to deal with stress is, as its name proposes, non-adaptive. It refers to using unhealthy or ineffective methods to deal with stress. These coping mechanisms may offer temporary relief, but they can negatively affect our well-being in the long run. We must recognize our coping methods and evaluate whether they genuinely benefit us.

It's crucial to take proactive steps toward adopting healthier strategies to break free from maladaptive coping patterns. Let's explore how you can accomplish this: Identify your maladaptive coping mechanisms:

1. Take a moment to reflect on your typical responses to stress and identify any patterns that may be counterproductive or harmful. For instance, let's say you tend to turn to excessive alcohol consumption to cope with work-related stress.

2. Understand the triggers and underlying reasons: Dive deeper into the catalysts and root causes that lead you to employ maladaptive coping mechanisms. For example, you may find that excessive alcohol consumption is triggered by overwhelming feelings and the need to escape work pressures.

3. Nurture self-awareness: Enhance your self-awareness by attentively observing your thoughts, emotions, and behaviors during stressful moments. Recognize the

negative impact of excessive alcohol consumption on your physical and mental well-being. Acknowledge how it may worsen stress levels and hinder your overall functioning.

4. Seek alternative coping strategies: Explore healthier and more effective coping strategies to replace your maladaptive ones. For instance, instead of resorting to alcohol, you could opt for regular physical exercise, practice relaxation techniques such as deep breathing or meditation, or confide in a trusted friend or family member for support.

5. Implement gradual changes: Introduce new coping strategies into your daily routine. Begin with small, manageable steps to prevent overwhelming yourself, and remember to celebrate your progress as you move forward. Celebrate your progress along the way. For instance, you may begin by incorporating a 10-minute meditation practice into your morning routine or dedicating specific daily time to physical exercise.

6. If you find it challenging to overcome maladaptive coping patterns, do not hesitate to seek support from a mental health professional. They can offer guidance, provide customized coping strategies, and assist you in navigating the change process.

This exercise aims to identify which strategies we consciously or unconsciously use to deal with stress are helpful and adaptive and those whose only consequence is to feed the stress cycle.

## LETTING GO OF PERFECT

I had high expectations for myself in my early years as an educator. Being the best teacher meant striving for perfection in my work. I meticulously planned my lessons, spent countless hours grading papers, and went above and beyond to create a nurturing classroom environment. On the surface, I was dedicated and committed. Yet, deep down, I was drowning in pursuing an unattainable ideal.

The pressure to be perfect added to the existing external stressors and took away the joy and fulfillment I once found in teaching. I perceived every minor setback as a personal failure, and I frequently doubted my abilities. I would spend endless nights agonizing over the tiniest mistakes, continually striving for an unattainable level of perfection. This relentless pursuit left me mentally and emotionally exhausted.

At the time, I failed to realize that perfectionism was detrimental to my well-being and harmed my students. My obsession with perfection overshadowed the genuine connections I could have built with them. I was so focused on meeting impossible standards that I overlooked each student's unique strengths and individual needs. I needed to take advantage of opportunities for growth and learning for myself and my students.

It took a significant turning point in my life for me to recognize the destructive nature of perfectionism and make a conscious decision to let go. I realized that being the best teacher did not mean being flawless or infallible. It meant embracing imperfections, learning from mistakes, and cultivating an environment that nurtured growth and authenticity.

By releasing the grip of perfectionism, I could reclaim my passion for teaching. I shifted my focus from unattainable standards to meaningful connections with my students. I embraced flexibility and experimentation in my teaching methods, allowing room for creativity and adaptation. I learned to celebrate my and my student's progress rather than fixating on perfection.

Perfectionism can be defined as a relentless pursuit of flawlessness and an unattainable ideal of perfection. People dealing with perfectionists have exceptionally high standards for themselves and are excessively critical of any perceived mistakes or shortcomings. They may constantly seek approval and validation from others, placing their self-worth on achieving perfection in various areas of their lives.

You may find yourself investing hours upon hours crafting the perfect lesson plan, meticulously considering every detail and aspect. You need help to delegate tasks or deviate from your meticulously outlined plan, fearing that any deviation may result in a less-than-perfect teaching experience, or you pressure your students to achieve top grades and meet exceptionally high standards. You find it challenging to accept anything less than perfection from them, often feeling disappointed or personally responsible when they don't meet your lofty expectations.

The underlying causes of perfectionism can vary from individual to individual. Factors contributing to its development include personal traits, upbringing, societal and cultural influences, and the desire for control and certainty. Perfectionism can also arise as a response to past experiences of criticism or failure, leading individuals to believe that perfection is the only way to avoid negative judgment.

While striving for excellence can have benefits, it is essential to be aware of the potential dangers of perfectionism. These obsessive tendencies can lead to chronic stress, anxiety, and diminished self-worth. Perfectionism can also impede personal growth, as the fear of failure and making mistakes may deter individuals from taking risks or embracing new opportunities.

Reflecting on my journey with perfectionism, I realize how deeply ingrained it was in my mindset and how it affected various aspects of my life, including my teaching career. I used to believe that unless everything was perfect, I wouldn't be able to earn the respect and approval of my colleagues, administrators, and even my students. I believed that working extra hours, going above and beyond, and never settling for anything less than perfection were the keys to success.

But over time, I began to realize that this mindset was unrealistic and detrimental to my well-being. The ongoing pressure to be flawless left me exhausted, anxious, and overwhelmed. It took a toll on my mental and emotional health, and I constantly strived for an unattainable standard.

Regardless, as I embarked on my journey of self-discovery and personal growth, I questioned the validity of my perfectionistic beliefs. I began to explore alternative ways of thinking and coping that would enable me to break free from the chains of perfectionism.

Letting go of perfectionism was a challenging process. It required self-reflection, self-compassion, and a willingness to challenge my limiting beliefs. I came to the realization that I needed to concentrate on what I could control and release the unrealistic expectations I had imposed upon myself. It was freeing to acknowledge that I couldn't control everything that occurred in my life. Still, I could hold how I responded to those situations.

Instead of constantly striving for perfection, I learned to celebrate progress and appreciate the growth from making mistakes. Being authentic and genuine in my interactions with colleagues, loved ones, and students created stronger connections and fostered a positive learning environment.

My intention with this book is to transmit to you all the knowledge I acquired through years of teaching and learning.

## What's Stressing You Out?

| Questions | Sample Answer | Your Answer |
| --- | --- | --- |
| **What changed during the isolation for you as a teacher?** | Transitioning to remote teaching was an important change requiring adaptation that I had to introduce to my lesson plans and finding new ways to engage students online. | |
| **What new challenges did you have to face?** | I had to learn how to interact with technology that I was not aware of, as well as address the varying home environments of the different students. | |

| | | |
|---|---|---|
| **How has stress impacted your well-being as a teacher?** | There was a significant amount of stress, which led to sleep disturbances and feeling exhausted. | |
| **Which coping strategies have you employed to manage job-related stress?** | Short breaks during the workday and mindfulness exercises helped reduce the stress. | |
| **Have you sought any external support or resources to address stress?** | Yes, I've contacted the school's counsel or to talk about stress management. | |
| **How has your school administration addressed safety concerns for teachers and staff?** | The school implemented safety protocols, such as improved security measures and staff training. | |
| **Have you experienced harassment or aggression from students or parents?** | There have been a few instances in which I have felt unsafe. I reported them to ensure a safe environment for everyone. | |
| **How do you advocate for a safe and respectful learning environment for yourself and your students?** | I often promote open communication and encourage a positive classroom culture. | |
| **Have you utilized any tutoring programs or additional support for struggling students?** | Yes, I have connected some students with tutoring programs to provide them with extra assistance. | |
| **How do you prioritize your mental health amidst a demanding teaching schedule?** | I always try to allocate time for self-care activities such as exercising or spending quality time with my loved ones. | |

| | | |
|---|---|---|
| **Have you advocated for additional resources or staffing to support the needs of your students and yourself as a teacher?** | Yes I have, to ensure a well-rounded education and a supportive work environment. | |
| **How do you intend to utilize your summer break to unwind and revitalize?** | I intend to go on vacation with my family. | |
| **Which self-care activities do you find most beneficial during the summer break?** | I like to spend time outdoors and do other creative activities, such as writing. | |
| **Have you made any professional development plans for the summer break to enhance your teaching skills?** | Yes, I've signed up for some online workshops and webinars to improve my teaching. | |

# 3
# IT IS OKAY TO ASK FOR HELP

*"We tap into something when we're honest about what's going on in our lives."*

— *SHERYL SANDBERG*

There was a period in my life when I reached a point of absolute despair. Burnout had consumed me, draining every ounce of energy and motivation. As a teacher, I took pride in my ability to handle everything adeptly. I held the belief that seeking help was a sign of weakness or incompetence. But little did I know my refusal to seek support would worsen my condition.

Ignoring the signs that I desperately needed help, my journey through burnout took a toll on my mental and physical health. The relentless stress, exhaustion, and emotional strain slowly eroded my well-being. Day by day, I pushed myself to the limit, convinced I could soldier on independently. I thought I was strong, resilient, and self-reliant, but I couldn't have been more wrong.

The consequences of my stubbornness became painfully apparent as my condition deteriorated. As it progressed, burnout led to other mental and physical health issues. My productivity plummeted, my relationships suffered, and I lost touch with the joy and passion that once fueled my work. It was a wake-up call, a stark reminder that I was only human and that my well-being mattered.

Amidst this difficult period, I learned a valuable lesson: It's perfectly fine to ask for help. This realization, though initially difficult to accept, opened the door to a path of healing and growth. I started to grasp that seeking assistance wasn't an indication of weakness but rather a display of strength and self-care. Everyone needs support and guidance, regardless of profession or background.

I invite you to ask for help and accept support from a loved one or a professional. We will explore the notion that seeking help is not a sign of failure but rather a courageous step towards self-improvement and well-being.

We all experience moments when we need someone to lean on, someone to lend a listening ear or a helping hand. And that's fine. We are social beings, and our commitment to ourselves today can also guide a loved one tomorrow.

## DON'T IGNORE THE SIGNS

Regarding our mental and emotional well-being, it's crucial to pay attention to the signs indicating we may need help. These signs can manifest in various ways, and awareness of them is the first step towards seeking the support and assistance we require. While everyone's experiences differ, some indicators suggest it's time to reach out for help.

Some of these indicators encompass enduring feelings of sadness, anxiety, or hopelessness. You might find yourself withdrawing from activities and relationships you once enjoyed, experiencing changes in appetite or sleep patterns, or feeling overwhelmed by daily tasks. Physical manifestations such as headaches, digestive issues, or unexplained aches and pains can also serve as indicators of underlying emotional distress. It is crucial to disregard these signs as transient or insignificant. Instead, they should serve as valuable cues that it's time to prioritize your well-being.

Why you need to be aware of why you feel that way: Understanding the underlying reasons behind your emotions and behaviors is essential for your overall well-being. It's like navigating a map—when you know your starting point and destination, it becomes easier to choose the right path.

Knowing why you're feeling a certain way helps you identify patterns, triggers, and potential stressors in your life. It enables you to attain clarity and perspective, empowering you to take suitable action. Try to pinpoint the sources of your distress, whether they stem from work, relationships, personal expectations, or other factors, so you can take steps to address them effectively. It's a process of self-discovery and self-compassion that leads to personal growth and improved well-being.

Acknowledging your emotions and understanding their causes does not make you weak or flawed. On the contrary, it demonstrates strength and self-awareness. Through this awareness, you can pave the way for positive change and embark on a journey of healing and self-care.

Recognizing that we need help can be one of the most challenging tasks to undertake. Several factors contribute to this difficulty, including toxic positivity, toxic masculinity (when it comes to men), and the social stigma surrounding mental health. Nonetheless, it is crucial to acknowledge that these obstacles can be surmounted, and seeking support is a demonstration of strength and self-care.

Toxic positivity is a mindset that promotes the idea of always being positive and happy, even in the face of difficulties. While optimism has merits, toxic positivity dismisses and invalidates negative emotions, making it difficult for individuals to express their struggles openly. This fosters an unrealistic expectation that we must always remain strong and cheerful, leaving little space for vulnerability or seeking assistance. For example, a person may feel pressured to put on a brave face and downplay their struggles, fearing that admitting their challenges will be a sign of weakness.

Toxic masculinity, specifically affecting men, perpetuates that seeking help or showing vulnerability is unmanly. Men are frequently conditioned to repress their emotions and uphold a stoic demeanor, making it exceedingly challenging for them to seek help when needed. This societal expectation puts undue pressure on men to handle everything independently, even when overwhelmed or struggling. Consequently, they might be reluctant to seek support, fearing judgment or a perceived loss of masculinity.

Furthermore, throughout history, the social stigma linked to mental health has deterred numerous individuals from seeking assistance. However, it's encouraging that new generations are increasingly questioning and challenging this stigma. Increased awareness and comprehension of mental health have paved the way to more candid discussions and enhanced societal acceptance. Nevertheless, the fear of being labeled as "weak" or facing discrimination can still deter individuals from seeking the help they need.

Asking for help can be daunting, which often evokes feelings of vulnerability and hesitation. We live in a society that celebrates independence and self-reliance, where seeking assistance can sometimes be seen as a sign of weakness. However, the psychological reasons behind our struggle to ask for help run deeper than societal norms.

Research has shown several factors regarding the difficulty of asking for help (Robbins, 2020). One of these aspects pertains to the fear of appearing incompetent or inadequate. Reaching out for assistance might be perceived as a sign of our shortcomings or an admission of failure. This fear stems from our desire to maintain a positive self-image and avoid potential judgment or criticism from others.

One more psychological obstacle revolves around the notion that we ought to manage everything Independently. We often internalize the notion that asking for help is a burden to others or an indication of our inability to cope. This self-imposed pressure to be self-sufficient can prevent us from reaching out when we need support.

Overcoming the barriers to asking for help requires courage and self-compassion. Here are some tips and advice to support you in this process:

- Challenge the narratives: Acknowledge that seeking help is an indication of strength, not weakness. Replace self-judgment with self-compassion and recognize that it takes courage to ask for assistance.
- Normalize seeking help: Understand that everyone faces challenges and needs support at different times. Remind yourself that seeking help is an inherent part of human experience.
- Surround yourself with a supportive network: Nurture connections with individuals who validate your emotions and encourage seeking help. Cultivate a supportive community that fosters open communication and understanding.
- Start with baby steps: Begin by reaching out to a trusted friend, family member, or professional. By opening up and sharing your thoughts and feelings with someone, you can establish a safe and supportive space to seek guidance and support.
- Educate yourself: Familiarize yourself with mental health and the advantages of seeking help. Understanding its positive impact on your well-being can motivate you to overcome any lingering doubts or fears.

Look for communities and support networks where you feel accepted, understood, and supported. Being surrounded by people who empathize with your struggles and uplift your well-being can make a difference. Additionally, don't underestimate the value of consulting with a mental health professional. They have the expertise and experience to guide you through your challenges, provide personalized strategies, and help you develop effective coping mechanisms.

Contrary to the belief that asking for help is a sign of weakness, research suggests that it can enhance our work performance and overall well-being (Robbins, 2020). When we ask for support, we tap into the collective wisdom and resources of others, enabling us to gain new perspectives, insights, and skills.

Engaging in seeking assistance can promote collaboration and teamwork, fostering a supportive environment where individuals feel valued and empowered. It promotes a culture of trust and mutual support, allowing for greater creativity, innovation, and problem-solving within organizations.

Moreover, asking for help can alleviate the overwhelming burden of trying to do everything independently. It frees up mental and emotional space, enabling us to focus on tasks and responsibilities that align with our strengths and expertise.

This act of courage and self-love will open doors to personal and professional growth for you. It will make you cultivate a sense of humility, empathy, and resilience. Most importantly, you acknowledge that your well-being and success depend not solely on your efforts but also on the support and collaboration of those around you.

Discovering help and support does not follow a one-size-fits-all approach. Communicating your needs to the trusted person or organization you contact is essential. Everyone's circumstances and requirements are unique, and expressing what you need ensures that you receive the most appropriate assistance and support.

Apart from seeking help from trusted individuals, there are various organizations and helplines available to offer support and resources. Here are some reputable organizations and their contact details:

- **American Psychological Association Crisis Hotlines:** The APA Crisis Hotlines offer immediate assistance and support for individuals experiencing crises. They can provide guidance, resources, and appropriate mental health services referrals. Visit their website for more information: www.apa.org/topics/crisis-hotlines

- **Anxiety U.K.:** It is a charity organization dedicated to helping those with anxiety disorders. They offer a helpline and other services that provide support, information, and resources for managing anxiety. Learn more about their helpline services on their website: www.anxietyuk.org.uk/get-help/helpline-services/

- **Substance Abuse and Mental Health Services Administration:** SAMHSA is a U.S. government agency that provides assistance and resources for mental health and substance abuse concerns. Their National Helpline offers confidential and free round-the-clock support for individuals and families dealing with mental health or substance use disorders. Contact them through their website: www.samhsa.gov/find-help/national-helpline

- **Postpartum Depression and Anxiety:** Postpartum depression and anxiety can be challenging for new parents. The Maternal Mental Health Hotline and Postpartum Support International provide helpline services, resources, and support for individuals experiencing postpartum mental health difficulties. Reach out to them for assistance: mchb.hrsa.gov/national-maternal-mental-health-hotline and www.postpartum.net/

- **National Suicide Prevention Lifeline:** This 24/7 helpline is accessible in the United States. It offers free and confidential support to individuals in crisis or those worried about someone's well-being. Please find more information on their website: www.fcc.gov/988-suicide-and-crisis-lifeline

- **National Alliance on Mental Illness (NAMI):** NAMI is a grassroots mental health organization that offers support, education, and advocacy for individuals impacted by mental health conditions. They provide helpline services and resources to assist individuals and families. Visit their website to access their helpline: www.nami.org/help

- **National Child Traumatic Stress Network:** Offers resources, support, and aid for children and families who have encountered traumatic events. Their website offers information and a helpline to help individuals find appropriate services and support: www.nctsn.org/about-us/contact-us/get-help-now

- **The Trevor Project:** A prominent organization that provides crisis intervention and suicide prevention services to LGBTQ+ youth. They offer a helpline, text, and chat services to support needy individuals. Reach out to them through their website: www.thetrevorproject.org/get-help/
- **National Center on Domestic Violence, Trauma & Mental Health:** This organization emphasizes the link between domestic violence, trauma, and mental health. They provide resources and support for survivors of domestic violence. Visit their website for more information: www.nationalcenterdvtraumamh.org/survivors/

WHAT DOES HELP LOOK LIKE TO YOU?

During my journey, I came to realize that I couldn't do it all by myself. I reached a point where my responsibilities and struggles became overwhelming, and I acknowledged that I needed help. It wasn't an easy admission, as I had always prided myself on being independent and self-reliant. However, I knew deep down that seeking support was crucial for my well-being.

By confiding your thoughts and feelings in someone, you can establish a secure environment to seek guidance and support. I expected to be provided with solutions or advice on overcoming my challenges. Instead, they listened. They held space for me to express my thoughts, emotions, and fears without judgment or interruption. And in that moment, I realized that sometimes, we truly need someone who can genuinely listen and empathize with our struggles.

Help comes in various forms, and it's essential to recognize that our needs can change depending on the situation. We sometimes crave practical solutions, guidance, or expert advice to navigate a specific issue. On other occasions, we long for someone who can listen with compassion, validate our feelings, and provide emotional support. Both types of help are valuable and necessary, but understanding which one we require at a given moment is vital.

As you seek help, it's essential to reflect on what kind of support you desire and communicate that with the people you trust. Some individuals excel at problem-solving and providing tangible solutions, while others possess the gift of listening and offering empathy. By expressing your needs, you can guide those around you to provide assistance that aligns with what you're truly seeking.

Help comes in different shapes and sizes. It's not about finding a one-size-fits-all solution but understanding your unique requirements and reaching out to the right individuals to offer the support you need. Whether it's a trusted friend, family member, mentor, or professional, the power of reaching out and connecting with others can make an immense difference in your well-being.

Imagine going through a challenging time at work, feeling overwhelmed and emotionally drained. Assistance in the form of emotional support can make a profound impact. It could be a friend who listens attentively without judgment as you share your thoughts and feelings. Their empathetic presence and comprehension can offer a feeling of validation and solace. You might also seek emotional support from a therapist or counselor who can provide professional guidance and help you navigate your emotions in a safe and confidential space.

When seeking emotional support, it's crucial to articulate your needs clearly. You can let your trusted friend or therapist know you're seeking someone to talk to, someone who can lend a compassionate ear and offer support. Be candid about your experiences and what you aspire to achieve through their support.

You can expect active listening, empathy, and validation when receiving emotional support. The person providing support is likely to offer a non-judgmental environment where you can freely express yourself. They may offer guidance, reassurance, and perspective, helping you gain clarity and cope with your emotions more effectively.

But here, I want to stop to make an important caveat: maybe you won't find the support you need in a loved one on the first try. In this situation, it is essential not to take it personally and understand that our friends and family want to help us. If they say or do something that doesn't help you, try to guide them to give you the support you need. Teach them to support you and help them to help you. Remember that other people cannot guess our needs; we must communicate with them effectively.

Now, let's consider a scenario where you're facing a demanding project deadline and feeling overwhelmed by the workload. Practical support can come to your aid in this situation. It might involve a colleague offering to share the workload by assisting you with specific tasks. They might lend a helping hand, allowing you to delegate some responsibilities and lighten your burden.

You can approach a trusted colleague or supervisor and explain the tasks you find challenging to handle alone. Be transparent about your limitations and communicate your readiness to collaborate and work together to achieve a common goal.

You can expect collaboration, teamwork, and shared responsibility when receiving practical support. The person providing support may help with specific tasks, share their expertise, or offer resources to facilitate project completion. Their assistance can alleviate your workload and contribute to a more balanced and successful outcome.

Having someone you trust in your support system can be invaluable for gaining a fresh perspective and realigning yourself with what truly matters. Trusted individuals, such as friends, family members, or even therapists, can offer a different viewpoint on your situation and help you see things from a new angle. Their insights and guidance can assist you in making decisions, overcoming challenges, and finding clarity in your life.

Now, let's explore some online therapy and counseling organizations and services that can provide professional support and guidance. These platforms provide convenient and accessible options for receiving treatment and counseling support.

- Talkspace is an online therapy platform that links individuals with licensed therapists through text, voice, and video messaging. It offers a flexible and confidential space to seek support and guidance for various mental health concerns. Through their secure and user-friendly platform, you can communicate with a licensed therapist at your convenience, making therapy accessible and convenient.

- BetterHelp is an online counseling platform that grants access to licensed therapists with expertise in diverse mental health domains. It offers private and secure text, chat, phone, and video communication. BetterHelp allows individuals to access professional counseling from the comfort of their own homes, offering flexibility and convenience.

- Amwell is a telehealth platform that offers online therapy services, allowing individuals to connect with licensed therapists through video sessions. It provides various healthcare services, including mental health support, making accessing professional help remotely more accessible. With Amwell, you can schedule virtual therapy sessions and receive personalized support from qualified therapists.

- ReGain is an online therapy platform designed for couples and relationship counseling. It connects individuals and couples with licensed therapists specializing in addressing relationship issues. ReGain offers a secure and confidential online space for couples to seek guidance, improve communication, and work through relationship challenges.

- Online-Therapy.com is an online counseling platform that provides therapy services for various mental health concerns. It offers a comprehensive approach to therapy, combining evidence-based techniques and interactive tools. Through Online-Therapy.com, you can access a range of therapeutic resources, including worksheets, messaging with therapists, and live sessions.

These online therapy and counseling organizations offer accessible and professional support for individuals seeking guidance, coping strategies, and mental health services. They provide a convenient way to connect with licensed therapists, enabling you to access help from the comfort of your own space and according to your schedule. Each platform has its unique approach and features, so it's essential to explore their websites to understand how they work and determine which aligns best with your needs.

## It Is Okay to Ask For Help

| Questions | Sample Answer | Your Answer |
| --- | --- | --- |
| **Pause and reflect on a moment when you felt overwhelmed and hesitated to ask for help. What were the reasons behind your hesitation? How could accepting support have improved the situation?** | There are times where I have a heavy workload and I avoid asking for help because I don't want to appear incapable. However, asking for help would have lightened the burden and prevented burnout. | |
| **Share a personal story about a teacher who initially resisted seeking help but later embraced it, leading to positive changes in their work-life balance.** | I had colleagues who struggled alone for a long time. When they sought help, they regained enthusiasm for teaching. | |
| **Write down three specific situations where you might need assistance managing work and life and commit to asking for help in at least one.** | Balance multiple projects, Handle challenging students, Manage stress. | |

| | |
|---|---|
| **Reflect on how seeking help is an indication of strength rather than weakness. Think about successful people you admire and how they might have relied on support to achieve their goals.** | Seeking help is a sign of strength and not a sign of weakness. |
| **Engage in a conversation with a colleague or friend about the importance of asking for help and share experiences of how it has benefited both of you.** | A colleague and I discussed how asking for help can improve our work and well-being. |
| **Make inquiries into your own personal barriers that hinder asking for help. Are they based on fear of judgment, perceived inadequacy, or something else?** | Some of my barriers include fear of judgment and desire to appear self-sufficient. Acknowledging these help me address them. |
| **Provide real-life scenarios of teachers who confronted their psychological barriers and found empowerment in seeking assistance.** | A teacher overcame fear of judgment, asked for help, and discovered a supportive community. Because of this, they improved their teaching. |
| **Create a list of strategies to address your specific psychological barriers and commit to trying at least one.** | 1. Practice self-compassion. 2. Normalize asking for help. 3. Communicate openly about challenges. |
| **Consider how vulnerability can foster stronger connections with others and how open communication can lead to mutual support.** | Sometimes, being vulnerable builds trust and connect you to others. While open communication makes sure everyone understands each other's needs and supports each other. |

| | | |
|---|---|---|
| **Share tips from experienced educators on how they have effectively communicated their needs to others.** | Be clear about your needs and express gratitude since that's a big part of communication. | |
| **Practice being vulnerable with someone you trust, expressing your challenges and the support you require.** | One time I opened up to a colleague about some of my struggles and their acknowledgment and understanding showed me the power of vulnerability. | |
| **Reflect on how seeking help can positively impact your well-being and effectiveness as a teacher.** | Seeking help decreases the stress you feel and improves how effective you are as a teacher. | |
| **Consider the different support networks available to you, both within and outside the workplace.** | Support networks can include family and friends, but also mentors and colleagues. What is important here is identifying these connections. | |
| **Provide a list of potential support sources and their respective roles in a teacher's life.** | 1. colleagues for work-related advice<br>2. mentors for career advice<br>3. friends and family for emotional support | |
| **Consider how mental health resources and helplines can be valuable support tools for teachers.** | Mental health resources can offer you vital support for teachers when facing different challenges. | |
| **Reflect on how help can manifest, from emotional encouragement to practical task assistance.** | Help can come in various forms, such as a listening ear or through practical assistance. | |
| **Reach out to a colleague and offer emotional or practical assistance, depending on their needs.** | For example, I offer emotional support to colleagues dealing with complicated situations, but the most important thing is being available. | |

# 4

## BACK TO SQUARE ONE

In this chapter, we will step back and reexamine the essence of who we are as teachers. It's time to revisit our roots, reignite that spark that led us into this noble profession, and reaffirm our purpose as educators.

Before we dive in, let's take a moment to reflect on something truly remarkable—the importance of teachers in society. Think about it: teachers are the backbone of education, the guiding lights that shape the minds of future generations. From teaching the basics of reading and writing to imparting essential life skills, educators hold the power to influence and inspire young minds like no one else.

But let me ask you this: When did you last pause to ponder your role as a teacher and its impact on your students' lives? Have you ever stopped to think about the incredible difference you make, academically and in shaping their character and molding their dreams?

Sometimes, we get so caught up in the daily grind that we forget our profound influence on our students' lives. We start questioning ourselves, wondering if we're doing enough, making a difference, or teaching is genuinely for us.

I can deeply empathize with this experience. Not long ago, I went above and beyond in my work, put in countless hours, and poured my heart and soul into my teaching. But despite my best efforts, I became emotionally exhausted and on the brink of burnout. It was a wake-up call that made me reassess my approach to teaching and my understanding of self-care.

As I looked back on my journey, I realized that I had lost sight of why I became a teacher in the first place. It wasn't just about imparting knowledge but nurturing a passion for learning, fostering creativity, and guiding my students to become compassionate, responsible, and confident individuals.

So, if you question your path or feel drained by the demands of teaching, know that you are not alone. It's okay to take a moment to reflect and realign with your purpose. Throughout this chapter, we will explore how to recapture the joy of teaching, reconnect with your calling, and embrace a renewed sense of fulfillment.

## HOW DO YOU KNOW?

As I embarked on rediscovering my purpose as a teacher, I knew that I couldn't do it alone. The time had come to be vulnerable and share my feelings with the people closest to me: my loved ones. Talking to them allowed me to gain a fresh perspective. It provided the support I needed to navigate through the doubts and uncertainties that clouded my mind.

But before I delve into the powerful conversations I had, let's take a moment to explore the concept of purpose in life. What is the purpose, and why is it crucial for our well-being?

Purpose can be seen as a guiding force that gives our lives meaning, direction, and significance. It's why we get out of bed each morning, the driving force behind our actions and the core of our passions and values. Having a clear sense of purpose is essential for our mental and emotional well-being.

Research shows that individuals with a strong sense of purpose tend to experience greater life satisfaction, overall happiness, and a reduced risk of mental health issues (Kim et al., 2020). A distinct purpose enhances our motivation, resilience, and ability to conquer challenges.

What makes purpose thrilling is its capacity to evolve and change over time. As we go through different life stages, our priorities and goals may shift, leading us to reevaluate our purpose and realign with what truly matters to us. This process of self-discovery is a continuous journey, and it's natural for our sense of purpose to grow and transform with us.

Now, let's explore some intriguing insights from the study on purpose in life conducted by the Greater Good Science Center at UC Berkeley (Science of Happiness Podcast, 2023). One notable finding was that purpose in life tends to grow with time and age. As we accumulate experiences and wisdom, we better understand ourselves and what truly fulfills us.

Moreover, education plays a significant role in shaping our sense of purpose. According to the study, individuals with higher levels of education tend to possess a stronger sense of purpose. This could be because education opens doors to new perspectives, opportunities, and passions, leading to a greater understanding of fulfillment and purpose.

Interestingly, while our neighborhood and environment can influence our well-being, the study showed that it makes only a tiny difference in our sense of purpose. Instead, our purpose in life is more strongly influenced by internal factors, such as our values, passions, and the people we surround ourselves with.

As I began my conversations with my loved ones, I realized the incredible benefits of having a purpose in life. Their unwavering support, empathy, and encouragement lifted my spirits. It helped me rediscover the deeper reasons why I became a teacher. Talking to them reinforced my love for teaching and reignited my passion for guiding and inspiring young minds.

Through my experiences, I discovered that having a sense of purpose not only enhances our own well-being but also creates a ripple effect on those around us. When aligned with our goals, we become better educators, partners, friends, and role models. It allows us to radiate positivity and impact the lives of others in ways we might not even realize.

I immersed myself in these conversations and discovered that my teaching purpose went beyond academic achievements. It was about nurturing confidence, compassion, and resilience in my students. It was about empowering them to embrace their individual strengths and create a positive impact in the world.

Rediscovering your objective as a teacher can be a journey that rekindles your passion and revitalizes your joy in the classroom. It's about peeling back the layers of external influences and reconnecting with the authentic reasons that led you to this noble profession in the first place. Below are some tips to assist you on this journey of self-discovery:

- **Reflect on your beginnings**: Take a moment to travel back in time and revisit the initial spark that ignited your desire to become a teacher. What inspired you, then? Was it the joy of seeing young minds flourish? Or the fulfillment derived from making a positive impact on the next generation? Think back to the time when you first considered becoming a teacher. Perhaps you were inspired by a mentor, a personal experience, or a deep desire to make a difference in the lives of young learners. Revisiting those initial motivations can clarify your true purpose as an educator.

- **Embrace your unique talents**: Recognize and celebrate the strengths and skills that make you an exceptional and effective teacher. Consider the unique qualities you bring to your classroom that set you apart. Each teacher brings their distinct strengths to the school. Whether you can foster creativity, cultivate empathy, or connect with students personally, embrace these talents as they contribute to your sense of purpose and impact as a teacher.

- **Embrace alignment with your core values**: They serve as act as guiding principles, shaping your decisions and actions. Reflect on the essential values and consider how your teaching aligns with these beliefs. Discover the values that deeply resonate with you, such as integrity, compassion, or lifelong learning. Evaluate how your teaching practices align with these values and consider adjusting to ensure your classroom reflects your authentic beliefs.

- **Embrace growth and change**: Recognize that purpose is not a fixed destination but rather an evolving journey. As you grow and evolve, your objective may also shift and expand. Teaching is a dynamic profession, and growth is a constant part of the journey. Embrace opportunities for professional development, explore innovative teaching methods, and be open to evolving as an educator to align with your ever-changing purpose.

- **Free yourself from the illusion of others**: It's essential to release yourself from the expectations and opinions of others. Always remember that your goal is personal and distinctive to you. Don't let external judgments cloud your understanding of why you teach and what fulfills you. Release the desire for external validation and refrain from comparing yourself with other educators. Trust your abilities and focus on your progress in nurturing your students' growth and potential.

Being a teacher is a multifaceted and demanding role that requires constant daily communication and interaction with diverse individuals. From students with varying learning styles and personalities to parents with unique expectations, navigating these interactions is undoubtedly rewarding and challenging. As educators, we are entrusted with guiding and nurturing young minds, which often comes with its fair share of complexities.

Amidst the array of personalities and expectations, it becomes essential for teachers to be self-aware—knowing their strengths and weaknesses and embracing them equally. Recognizing and accepting our strengths empowers us to leverage these qualities to create engaging and effective learning environments. Whether we can foster creativity, empathize with students, or simplify complex concepts, these strengths contribute significantly to our sense of purpose and direction as educators.

Simultaneously, acknowledging our weaknesses with kindness and self-compassion is equally vital. As teachers, we are not infallible, and it's okay to have areas where we may need improvement. Embracing our vulnerabilities allows us to grow personally and professionally, seeking continuous development and refining our teaching methods to better serve our students' needs.

By being self-aware and accepting our pros and cons, we can better understand ourselves and our purpose. Instead of feeling overwhelmed by the challenges that come our way, we can approach each situation with confidence and resilience. Embracing our authentic selves fosters a positive sense of self, directly translating into a more fulfilling teaching experience.

Moreover, awareness of our strengths and weaknesses helps us develop a more comprehensive support system. Collaborating with colleagues with complementary strengths can create a symbiotic teaching environment where teachers can learn from one another, share insights, and collectively enhance their abilities.

Ultimately, as we navigate the complexities of being a teacher, self-awareness, and self-acceptance become potent tools for strengthening our sense of purpose, direction, and identity in the ever-evolving world of education. Embracing our unique selves enables us to make a lasting impact on our students' lives, foster a positive learning atmosphere, and find fulfillment in the noble journey of education.

## RE-ESTABLISHING WHO YOU ARE

In our pursuit of rediscovering our purpose as teachers, one powerful tool emerges self-awareness. As educators, navigating diverse environments daily, understanding the concept of self-awareness and its significance becomes vital in shaping our personal and professional lives.

So, what exactly is self-awareness? It goes beyond merely recognizing our reflection in a mirror; it involves delving into our thoughts, emotions, and behaviors across various situations. This inward exploration grants us valuable insights into our strengths, weaknesses, values, and beliefs, enabling us to make better-informed decisions, improve relationships, and foster personal growth.

When we talk about this, we find two primary states: internal and external self-awareness. The first pertains to understanding our emotions, preferences, and character traits. For instance, I faced a challenging parent-teacher meeting, where frustration and defensiveness clouded my judgment, preventing constructive communication and problem-solving.

On the other hand, external self-awareness comes into play when we recognize how others perceive us. I experienced this when a colleague approached me to discuss my classroom management approach. Their feedback illuminated how my teaching style might impact student engagement and learning.

This brings us to the question of why self-awareness matters so much. The answer lies in its potential to unlock our true potential. By comprehending our strengths and weaknesses, we can leverage our abilities and focus on areas that require growth. In the context of teaching, this cultivates a more positive and nurturing learning environment for our students.

Moreover, self-awareness enhances our ability to empathize and connect effectively. As teachers, this skill is invaluable in our interactions with students, parents, colleagues, and school administrators. Understanding our emotional responses and how others perceive us fosters more meaningful and authentic relationships, making us more impactful educators.

Self-awareness is a potent tool that aids us in comprehending our inner selves and what motivates us. It is a journey of introspection and self-discovery, essential for personal growth and finding our purpose in life. The development of this skill encompasses multiple facets that enable us to gain insights into our thoughts, emotions, and behaviors.

One way to develop self-awareness is by recognizing the different levels of self-awareness we can experience. The first level is essential, where we become aware of our feelings and reactions in different situations. For example, as an educator, I noticed that specific classroom scenarios would trigger stress and frustration while others brought joy and fulfillment. By acknowledging these emotions, I could start identifying patterns and areas that needed attention.

The second level is self-awareness through self-reflection. This involves actively exploring our thoughts, beliefs, and values. It's like peering into a mirror to understand our true desires and motivations. As for me, I turned to journaling to contemplate my experiences as a teacher. This practice revealed my passion for positively impacting my students' lives. It showed areas where I needed to grow and evolve.

It's essential to understand the distinction between self-consciousness and self-awareness. While both may sound similar, each a distinct characteristic. Self-consciousness is a state where we are excessively aware of how others perceive us, often leading to anxiety and self-doubt. On the other hand, self-awareness focuses on understanding ourselves without judgment, acknowledging our strengths, and embracing our imperfections. I recall moments when I was self-conscious about my teaching style, constantly seeking validation from others. However, self-awareness taught me to trust my abilities and find my approach authentic.

The benefits of self-awareness are plentiful and directly impact both our personal and professional lives. By cultivating self-awareness, we can make intentional decisions that align with our values and goals. This clarity allows us to establish healthy boundaries, prioritize tasks effectively, and navigate challenging situations with composure. Moreover, self-awareness fosters empathy and understanding toward others, enhancing our interpersonal relationships and communication skills.

To develop self-awareness, consider the following pieces of advice:

1. **Incorporate mindfulness practices**: Engaging in techniques like meditation or deep breathing exercises can enhance your awareness of thoughts and emotions. They enable you to observe without judgment, making it easier to recognize triggers and responses.

2. **Request feedback from others**: Approach trusted friends, colleagues, or mentors and inquire about their honest assessment of your strengths and areas for growth. Being receptive to diverse perspectives can provide valuable insights.

3. **Maintain a reflective journal**: Consistently record your experiences, emotions, and reflections. Reviewing your entries can unveil recurring patterns and emotional triggers, helping you better understand yourself. If you're unsure how to begin, there is no need to worry. Below, I'll provide you with some recommendations.

4. **Practice active listening**: Be attentive to your responses while engaging in conversations with others. This practice aids in developing a greater awareness of your communication style and emotional responses.

5. **Embrace vulnerability**: Permit yourself to be open and receptive to self-discovery. Assuming your imperfections and acknowledging areas for improvement is a decisive step toward growth.

No two days are the same on the journey of self-awareness. Some days may be more complex than others as we face challenges and uncertainties that test our resilience and sense of self.

Being patient with ourselves during these times is crucial. Progress may sometimes feel slow, but even small steps are significant.

Dear reader, as you continue your journey of self-awareness and rediscover your purpose as a teacher, I want to introduce you to a powerful tool that can accompany you every step: the journal. Journaling is a personal and reflective practice that can help you unlock the depths of your thoughts, emotions, and aspirations. It is a safe space to freely explore your experiences and gain valuable insights into your identity and what truly matters to you.

Journaling goes beyond pen and paper; it's a gateway to self-discovery and a deeper connection with yourself. Through journaling, you can:

- **Develop self-awareness**: As you put your thoughts into words, you become more conscious of your feelings, reactions, and thought patterns. Journaling encourages exploring your inner world, paving the way to self-awareness and understanding.
- **Recognize your purpose**: Journaling allows you to reflect on your values, passions, and motivations. It will help you to identify recurring themes that may hint at your true purpose as an educator.
- **Unleash creativity**: Writing in a journal is a creative outlet that can spark innovative ideas and insights. It fosters thinking outside the box and encourages the exploration of new perspectives.
- **Manage stress**: Expressing your thoughts and emotions on paper can be cathartic, relieving the stresses of everyday life. It is akin to a mental

decluttering process that leaves you feeling lighter and more centered.

How to begin? Starting a journal is a simple yet powerful step toward self-awareness. Below is a step-by-step guide to help you in embarking on this journey:

1. **Find the right journal:** Choose a journal that resonates with you, whether a beautiful leather-bound notebook or a simple spiral-bound one. Opt for a journal that invites you to write and feels comfortable in your hands.
2. **Allocate time:** Set aside a few minutes each day for journaling. It can be in the morning to set intentions for the day or in the evening to reflect on your experiences.
3. **Establish a safe space:** Discover a serene and tranquil environment where you can concentrate without interruptions. Transform this space into your sanctuary for self-reflection and exploration.
4. **Start writing:** Commence with whatever thoughts come to your mind. Write about your thoughts, emotions, and experiences without judgment. Allow your words to flow freely and authentically.
5. **Take time to reflect on your journal entries:** Go through your previous journal entries to recognize any recurring patterns, emotions, and thoughts. This retrospective process can offer valuable insights into your journey of self-awareness.

To inspire and support you in your journaling journey, here are some prompts to assist you in delving deeper into your thoughts and emotions:

- Recount a moment in the classroom when you felt the greatest sense of fulfillment. What activity were you engaged in, and what aspect of it brought you joy?
- What are the current challenges you are encountering as a teacher? How do these challenges align with your values and purpose?
- Write a letter to your future self. Elaborate on your aspirations and goals as an educator and outline the steps you intend to take to achieve them.
- Reflect on a recent interaction with a student or colleague. What emotions stirred in you, and what insights did you acquire from the experience?
- Explore your teaching philosophy. What are your core beliefs and principles as an educator? How do they guide your actions in the classroom?

This is a personal and flexible practice. There are no right or wrong answers, only authentic reflections that lead you closer to your purpose and sense of self. As you embark on this journey of self-awareness, show kindness to yourself, and embrace any progress you make, regardless of how small it may seem.

# Back to Square One

| Questions | Sample Answer | Your Answer |
| --- | --- | --- |
| Pause for a moment and recall the initial spark that inspired you to become a teacher. How has your purpose evolved since then, and how has it impacted your motivation and fulfillment in your career? | My initial spark was the desire to make a difference. As time moved on, it developed into a commitment to grow a positive learning environment. | |
| Share a personal story about a teacher who went through a period of burnout but reignited their passion for teaching by reconnecting with their original purpose. | I had a colleague who was experiencing burnout but they recovered their passion by revisiting why they started teaching. | |
| Consider the ripple effect of your teaching on students, families, and communities. How does acknowledging this responsibility influence your commitment to self-awareness? | Having an understanding of the ripple effect can reinforce my commitment to self-awareness since it impacts the broader community beyond the classroom. | |
| Feature a testimonial from a student or former student who had a transformative experience with a teacher known for their self-awareness and empathetic approach. | Once a student shared how a self-aware teacher positively impacted their life and created a lasting impression of empathy and understanding. | |
| Reflect on how awareness of your internal thoughts and feelings influences how you present yourself externally. How do your internal and external self-awareness align, and in what areas do they differ? | Internal thoughts and awareness can shape my external interactions. Because of this, they align when I'm myself. | |

| | | |
|---|---|---|
| **How can you overcome these obstacles to cultivate a deeper level of self-awareness?** | Obstacles include time constraints. To overcome these, I have to schedule a dedicated reflection time every week and make it a habit within my routine. | |
| **Share practical reflection exercises or techniques other teachers use to promote self-awareness, such as keeping a weekly reflective journal.** | Teachers might find success in keeping reflective journals since it might help in identifying patterns and processing experiences. | |
| **How can acknowledging weaknesses become a source of power in your teaching journey?** | Acknowledging weaknesses allows for growth. It also transforms challenges into opportunities for improvement. | |
| **Highlight a teacher who initially struggled with accepting their weaknesses but found that doing so allowed them to seek help and collaborate with colleagues, resulting in improved teaching outcomes.** | A teacher's acceptance of weaknesses led to collaboration and seeking help, ultimately enhancing teaching outcomes and fostering a supportive environment. | |
| **Reflect on the advantages of journaling for self-discovery and how it can enhance your comprehension of your teaching experiences and emotions.** | Journaling offers a private space for reflection, which helps uncover patterns and gain insights into teaching experiences. | |
| **Reflect on the idea that personal growth is a gradual process. How can celebrating small victories along the way boost your self-awareness journey?** | Acknowledging small victories fuels motivation, reinforcing that personal growth is a journey, not a destination. | |
| **Offer a guided journaling prompt related to teaching experiences to help teachers explore their emotions and reactions in various situations.** | A prompt could be reflecting on a challenging classroom moment, where you can explore your emotions and actions, and consider any alternative responses to gain more understanding. | |

# 5

# SMARTER NOT HARDER

It's early morning, and you step into your classroom with a long to-do list. The school day begins, and you find yourself juggling lesson planning, grading, classroom management, meetings, parent-teacher interactions, and much more. The hours pass swiftly, leaving you feeling both accomplished and drained.

In this chapter, we dig into efficiency and effectiveness in teaching. We understand how demanding and time-consuming your role as an educator can be, which is why we aim to equip you with strategies to manage your responsibilities while maintaining a healthy work-life balance. Instead of working harder and feeling overwhelmed, it's time to work smarter.

As a teacher, your dedication to shaping young minds is commendable. Still, it's crucial to recognize that your well-being matters too. It is effortless to become entangled in the whirlwind of day-to-day responsibilities. Nevertheless, you might need to give greater consideration to self-care and personal development. Embracing a mindset of working smarter, not harder, empowers you to maximize your productivity while preserving your energy and enthusiasm for teaching.

Let's walk through a typical school day. You're already mentally organizing your schedule when you arrive on campus. Morning preparations involve setting up your classroom, reviewing lesson plans, and mentally preparing for the day's challenges. As the bell rings, you welcome your students, ready to engage them in a dynamic learning experience.

Throughout the day, you navigate between various tasks: guiding students through lessons, addressing questions, managing classroom dynamics, and offering emotional support. During breaks, you rush to the staff room to grab a coffee while grading assignments or responding to emails.

As the final bell rings, your day is far from over. There are meetings with colleagues, parent-teacher conferences, and professional development workshops. The workload may seem relentless, leaving little time for your well-being.

Now, imagine a different scenario where you work smarter. In this new approach, you prioritize tasks, focus on the most impactful activities, and implement strategies to streamline your workload. By recognizing the value of your time and energy, you create space for both professional growth and personal fulfillment.

In the upcoming sections, we will explore methods to enhance your efficiency, boost student engagement, and adapt to the evolving education landscape. We've covered you, from preparation techniques to embracing modern teaching platforms beyond the classroom. Let's embark on this journey together, where you'll rediscover the joys of teaching and experience the satisfaction of balancing your passion with self-care.

## PREPARATION IS KEY

Throughout history, education has been an ever-evolving process, adapting to the changing needs of societies and cultures. From the ancient civilizations of Mesopotamia and Egypt, where education was primarily reserved for the elite classes and passed down through oral traditions and apprenticeships, to the formal educational institutions that emerged over time, education has been fascinating and dynamic (Ghonge et al., 2020).

Comparing a 14th-century classroom to a modern one reveals stark differences in teaching methods and learning environments. In the 14th century, traditional classrooms were characterized by a teacher delivering lectures from the front. At the same time, students sat in rows, diligently taking notes. The teacher served as the sole source of knowledge, and the dissemination of information was often one-way (Simkin, J, 2020).

Fast-forward to the present day, when the internet has revolutionized education. With the advent of technology, classrooms have become more interactive and engaging. Teachers no longer rely solely on traditional textbooks and chalkboards; instead, they incorporate multimedia tools, interactive software, and online resources to enhance the learning experience.

Before the internet, educators played a crucial role as gatekeepers of knowledge. Their main duty was to impart information to their students and effectively manage the classroom. With limited access to information, teachers were the direct authority figures in the learning process.

However, the internet has disrupted this traditional model, empowering teachers and students. Educators now take on the role of facilitators, guiding students through a personalized learning journey. The abundance of online resources and digital platforms has democratized education, giving students access to a wealth of knowledge beyond the confines of the classroom.

Technology has become an invaluable tool for teachers, offering various benefits that enhance their effectiveness in the classroom. Online platforms and educational apps provide vast resources, from interactive lessons and virtual field trips to gamified learning experiences. These tools cater to diverse learning styles and interests, making education more inclusive and engaging.

Moreover, technology enables teachers to track student progress and provide timely feedback. Digital assessment tools simplify the grading process, allowing educators to allocate valuable time for instructional planning and providing individualized student support.

In the digital age, professional development opportunities have expanded beyond physical workshops and conferences. Educators can now participate in online webinars, collaborate with peers globally, and access rich educational content from reputable sources. The internet has created a vast network of educators who share best practices, ideas, and innovative teaching strategies.

As an educator, embracing technology and continuous learning is paramount. In today's fast-paced world, knowledge evolves rapidly, and new teaching methodologies emerge constantly. Stay updated with the latest trends and incorporate technology effectively to create dynamic and enriching learning environments for your students.

I've compiled a quick-reference online tool resource box that you can turn to whenever you need teaching resources to enrich your lessons and streamline administrative tasks.

## Khan Academy

- How it can help you: Khan Academy is a comprehensive platform that offers a wide range of free educational resources, including video lectures, practice exercises, and quizzes for various subjects and grade levels. It can supplement your teaching materials and offer personalized learning opportunities for your students.
- How to access it: Visit the website at www. khanacademy.org/.
- How to use it: Sign up as an educator and explore the vast library of resources. You can assign exercises and track your student's progress through the platform.

## Tynker

- How it can help you: Tynker is an interactive online learning platform designed to teach coding to students of all ages. It can be an excellent resource for integrating computer programming and computational thinking into your curriculum.
- How to access it: Access Tynker at www.tynker.com/.
- How to use it: Create a teacher account and explore the various coding lessons and activities available. You can monitor your students' coding progress and customize lessons to meet their needs.

## Wix Education

- How it can benefit you: Wix Education offers a user-friendly website builder that allows you to create a personalized classroom website. It serves as an excellent tool for sharing course materials, assignments, and resources with your students and their parents.
- How to access it: Access the platform at www.wix.com/education.
- How to use it: Create a free Wix account and choose from templates designed specifically for educators. Customize your website quickly and make it a communication and information dissemination hub.

## Canvas

- How it can help you: Canvas is a robust learning management system that simplifies course management, student communication, and assessment. It streamlines administrative tasks and facilitates seamless online learning experiences.
- How to access it: Visit Canvas at www.canvas.net/.
- How to use it: As an educator, you can leverage Canvas to create and organize course content, track student progress, and communicate with your class effectively. In addition to enriching your teaching resources, technology can also revolutionize your administrative tasks. Grading and evaluating students can be time-consuming, but by utilizing the appropriate tools, you can streamline these processes and allow you to concentrate more on teaching.

## Blackboard Instructor App

- How it can help you: The Blackboard Instructor App allows you to manage your courses and interact with students on the go. It provides quick access to essential course details and communication tools.
- How to access it: Download the app from your device's app store or visit www.blackboard.com/en-apac/ teaching-learning/learning-management/blackboard-instructor-app.
- How to use it: Log in with your Blackboard account, access your courses, grade assignments, and participate in discussions easily.

**Microsoft Excel**

- How it can help you: Microsoft Excel is a versatile spreadsheet tool that can simplify grade calculations and data management. It allows you to organize and analyze student data efficiently.
- How to access it: Excel is part of Microsoft Office Suite. Access it at www.microsoft.com/en-us/microsoft-365/excel.
- How to use it: Familiarize yourself with essential Excel functions, such as creating spreadsheets, entering grades, and using formulas to calculate averages.

**Google Sheets**

- How it can help you: Google Sheets is a cloud-based spreadsheet tool equipped with collaboration features. It is ideal for managing student progress and grades across multiple devices.
- How to access it: Access Google Sheets through your Google account or visit edu.google.com/intl/ALL_ph/for-educators/product-guides/sheets/?modal_active=none.
- How to use it: Learn how to create a Google Sheet, organize data, and utilize functions that automate grade calculations and data analysis.

## LEVEL UP THE ENGAGEMENT

As dedicated educators, we know that one of the most significant challenges we face is creating engaging lesson plans that align with the curriculum, capture our students' attention, and keep them excited about learning. Technology can be a game-changer when leveling up classroom engagement in today's digital age.

With the help of technology, we can integrate interactive elements into our lessons, making the learning experience more dynamic and enjoyable for our students. Online tools and platforms offer a wide range of resources that can support our teaching methods and enhance student participation.

Let's dive into our online tool resource box, where you can find quick and accessible resources to elevate Engagement in your classroom:

**Kahoot**

- How it can help you: Kahoot is a gamified learning platform that turns quizzes and assessments into exciting games. It promotes friendly competition and encourages active participation from every student.
- How to access it: Visit Kahoot at kahoot.com/.
- How to use it: Generate interactive quizzes or select from an extensive collection of pre-made Kahoots. Launch a Kahoot session in your classroom, and students can join using their devices to answer questions and earn points.

## Quizlet

- How it can help you: Quizlet is a versatile learning platform that offers a range of study tools, including flashcards, quizzes, and interactive games. It can assist students in reviewing and mastering course content in an engaging manner.
- How to access it: Access Quizlet at quizlet.com/.
- How to use it: Create custom study sets or explore existing sets created by other educators. Students can use flashcards and quizzes to reinforce their understanding of the material.

## Flippity

- How it can help you: Flippity is a free online tool that allows you to turn Google Sheets into interactive games, flashcards, and quizzes. It offers a unique way to engage your students with course material.
- How to access it: Access Flippity at www.flippity.net/.
- How to use it: Create a Google Sheet with your content and use Flippity's templates to convert it into interactive learning activities. Afterward, you can share the link with your students for them to enjoy.

By leveraging these online resources, you can add an element of excitement and interactivity to your lessons, making your classroom an engaging learning environment where students actively participate and retain knowledge better.

Technology empowers teachers to cater to diverse learning styles, adapt lessons to individual needs, and provide instant feedback. With these tools at your disposal, you can level up your engagement strategies and inspire a love for learning in your students, setting them up for success both in and outside the classroom.

## ADAPTING TO TEACHING PLATFORMS BEYOND THE CLASSROOM

In recent times, the landscape of education has witnessed a significant transformation due to the impact of COVID-19. Teachers had to adapt quickly to new teaching platforms beyond the traditional classroom. One of the most prevalent approaches during this time was hybrid teaching, combining face-to-face and online instruction elements.

Hybrid teaching differs from other instructional modes such as blended learning, remote education, and traditional face-to-face instruction. Blended learning typically integrates online and in-person instruction but may not necessarily involve concurrent teaching. Remote teaching is entirely online instruction, often during disruptions like the pandemic. On the other hand, mixed teaching consists of a combination of synchronous and asynchronous learning experiences, where students may attend in-person and virtual classes.

As educators, we've had to reimagine our teaching methods and adjust to accommodate physical and virtual learners in our classrooms. This has transformed the way we prepare and deliver our lessons. Taking advantage of online tools and resources can elevate the learning experience for all students.

Let's explore an online tool resource box, where you can find a variety of tools and management systems tailored to hybrid teaching and beyond.

## Google Classroom

- How it can help you: Google Classroom is a comprehensive platform that facilitates seamless communication, assignment distribution, and student collaboration in a virtual classroom environment.
- How to access it: Access Google Classroom at edu. google.com/intl/ALL_ph/workspace-for-education/ classroom/.
- How to use it: Organize and manage your classes, create and distribute assignments, and provide real-time feedback to your students.

## EdPuzzle

- How it can help you: EdPuzzle allows you to create interactive video lessons to engage and assess students' understanding of the content.
- How to access it: Access EdPuzzle at edpuzzle.com/.
- How to use it: Customize videos with questions and comments, track student progress, and gather insights on student performance.

## Nearpod

- How it can help you: Nearpod offers interactive lessons, virtual reality experiences, and formative assessments to keep students engaged during synchronous and asynchronous learning.
- How to access it: Access Nearpod at nearpod.com/.
- •How to use it: Create dynamic lessons with multimedia elements, collaborate with students, and gain real-time feedback.

## Showbie

- How it can help you: Showbie simplifies assigning, collecting, and providing feedback on assignments, making it an excellent tool for managing hybrid classrooms.
- How to access it: Access Showbie at www.showbie.com/.
- How to use it: Distribute assignments, provide audio and written feedback, and engage students in meaningful discussions.

## Flipgrid

- How it can help you: Flipgrid allows you to create video-based discussions, fostering a collaborative and inclusive learning environment.
- How to access it: Access Flipgrid at info.flip.com/en-us.html.

- How to use it: Pose questions or topics for discussion, and students respond with video responses, promoting Engagement and communication.

## Screencastify

- How it can help you: Screencastify enables you to create and share instructional videos, tutorials, and feedback with your students.
- How to access it: Access Screencastify at www.screencastify.com/.
- How to use it: Record your screen, webcam, or both, and easily share the videos with your students.

## Edublogs

- How it can help you: Edublogs provides a user-friendly platform for creating and maintaining class blogs, enhancing student communication and collaboration.
- How to access it: Access Edublogs at edublogs.org/.
- How to use it: Create class blogs for sharing resources, reflections, and student work.

## Jimdo

- How it can help you: Jimdo offers a simple website builder designed for teachers to create and manage their class websites.
- How to access it: Access Jimdo at www.jimdo.com/website/teacher/.

- How to use it: Design and customize your class website with essential information and resources for students and parents.

## ClassDojo

- How it can help you: ClassDojo is a versatile platform that facilitates communication, behavior management, and parent involvement.
- How to access it: Access ClassDojo at www.classdojo.com/.
- How to use it: Share class updates, photos, and videos with parents, and reward students for positive behavior.

## Seesaw

- Learn about its advantages: Seesaw is a student-driven digital portfolio that empowers students to demonstrate their learning and collaborate with peers.
- How to access it: Access Seesaw at web.seesaw.me/.
- How to use it: Students upload and share their work, and teachers provide feedback and assess their progress.

## Moodle

- How it can help you: Moodle is an open-source learning management system that supports personalized and collaborative learning experiences.

- How to access it: Access Moodle at moodle.org/?lang=pt.
- How to use it: Create and manage courses, engage students with interactive activities, and track their performance.

## Schoology

- How it can help you: Schoology is a powerful learning management system that streamlines course management and fosters student engagement.
- How to access it: Access Schoology at www. powerschool.com/classroom/schoology-learning/.
- How to use it: Organize and distribute course materials, communicate with students, and facilitate discussions.

## Padlet

- How it can help you: Padlet offers an interactive platform for collaboration, brainstorming, and sharing ideas among students.
- How to access it: Access Padlet at padlet.com/premium/ backpack.
- How to use it: Create virtual bulletin boards to collect student contributions and foster creativity.

## Webnode

- How it can help you: Webnode allows you to easily create simple and visually appealing class websites to share information and resources.
- How to access it: Access Webnode at www.webnode.com/.
- How to use it: Customize your class website with text, images, and multimedia to engage students and parents.

## Strikingly

- How it can help you: Strikingly provides a platform to create beautiful one-page websites perfect for showcasing student projects and achievements.
- How to access it: Access Strikingly at www.strikingly.com/?utm_source=nav&utm_medium=blog.
- How to use it: Design and easily publish student portfolios or class websites.

With these valuable online tools and resources, we teachers can confidently navigate the hybrid teaching landscape, delivering engaging lessons and fostering interactive learning experiences for in-person and virtual students. Embracing technology empowers us to adapt to the evolving educational landscape while providing our students the support and resources they need to succeed.

## Smarter Not Harder

| Questions | Sample Answer | Your Answer |
| --- | --- | --- |
| In what ways can technology enhance your work-life balance as a teacher? | Integrating technology can automate routine tasks, streamline communication, and provide flexibility in lesson planning, giving more time for personal and professional pursuits. | |
| How can online tools gamify lessons and encourage active student participation? | Online tools like Kahoot! can turn assessments into games, which fosters a fun and engaging learning environment. | |
| How can the time saved by using technology for grading be better utilized to improve teaching strategies? | With automated grading, teachers can invest time in personalized feedback, or refining their lesson plans. | |
| What advantages can hybrid teaching offer in meeting diverse learning needs, and how can it be effectively managed? | Hybrid teaching combines in-person and online methods, accommodating different learning styles and providing flexibility. | |
| How does incorporating multimedia elements into lesson plans enhance student understanding and retention? | Multimedia elements like videos cater to varied learning preferences, which make lessons more engaging for students. | |
| What benefits can regularly updating your knowledge of educational technology bring to teaching practices? | Staying up-to-date allows teachers to adopt new tools and techniques, which foster innovation and the outcome of students. | |

| | | |
|---|---|---|
| **Why is it convenient to have a well-curated collection of online tools for teaching needs?** | A well-curated collection of online tools with different purposes can create interactive content to assess students' progress. | |
| **How can technology ease the transition to hybrid teaching, and what steps can be taken to set up a digital classroom effectively?** | Well, technology facilitates seamless communication and content sharing, so setting up a digital classroom involves choosing a reliable platform and establishing clear guidelines. | |

# Battling Burnout in Teaching

*"Self-compassion is simply giving the same kindness to ourselves that we would give to others."*

— *CHRISTOPHER GERMER*

Burnout is a common problem in the modern world, but its prevalence in the teaching profession is nothing short of shocking. Research by WordsRated estimated that over 300,000 teachers in public schools quit between 2020 and 2022 because of burnout, and 64% of teaching staff said that they were "emotionally and physically exhausted" by the end of every school day.

That's a terrible statistic for a job that we do because we're passionate about it. At its best, teaching is exciting, rewarding, and inspiring. It leaves us energized and ready to go home and live our personal lives with enthusiasm. But at its worst, the opposite is true. We struggle to control our classes, the workload piles up, and we go home exhausted and unable to give our best to our families.

I've felt the pressure of burnout, and I've witnessed it in countless other teachers. I'm passionate about helping as many people in the profession as I can take care of themselves and implement strategies that allow them to give their best to the profession without sacrificing their health or happiness. That's why I wrote this book; it's why you're here reading it, and it's why I'd like to ask for your help in reaching more teachers.

**By leaving a review of this book on Amazon, you'll show other teaching staff where they can find the support they're looking for to take care of themselves in this challenging profession.**

Simply by letting other readers know how this book has helped you and what they'll find inside, you'll help them find the guidance they're looking for.

Thank you so much for your support. Together, we can bring that troublesome statistic down.

# 6

# NAVIGATING THE CLASSROOM

Imagine you're in a classroom with 1st to 10th graders. Would you consider teaching algebra to 1st graders? Or teaching the alphabet to 10th graders? The idea might seem challenging and impractical.

Indeed, we all recognize the importance of tailoring our curriculum to match each grade level's specific needs and learning abilities. In the same way, we must be tuned to the diverse types of learners in our classroom.

You see, every student learns uniquely. Some are visual learners, grasping information best through images and graphs. Others are auditory learners, benefiting most from spoken words and lectures. Then, some kinesthetic learners thrive through hands-on activities and movement.

Understanding and embracing these different learning styles is akin to having a superpower as an educator. By adapting our teaching strategies to accommodate the various types of learners, we can create a more engaging and practical learning experience for every student.

Throughout this chapter, we'll explore the four primary types of learners, discuss ways to adjust your teaching methods to suit each learner's preferences and navigate the art of handling conversations with challenging parents. My aim is to provide you with insights and practical tips to help you become an even more exceptional teacher. The

## FOUR TYPES OF LEARNERS

In this section, we explore the captivating realm of learning styles. It explores how they shape how our students absorb and retain information. Understanding the four primary types of learners—visual, auditory, read/write, and kinesthetic—will equip you with consequential insights to effectively teach each student with diverse learning preferences.

First, let's clarify what a learning style is. A learning style refers to an individual's preferred method of processing and understanding information. These styles are influenced by a blend of factors, which may include genetics, environment, and past experiences. As teachers, recognizing and accommodating these preferences can significantly impact our student's learning journey.

The VARK Model is a well-known framework that classifies learners into four primary categories:

- **Visual learners**: These people grasp information best through visual aids like charts, graphs, images, and videos. Consider incorporating colorful visual presentations and interactive materials to effectively teach visual learners. Utilize visual cues to emphasize key points and encourage students to create mind maps or concept diagrams to reinforce their understanding.
- **Auditory learners** thrive on spoken information and benefit most from lectures, discussions, and audio materials. To engage auditory learners, incorporate verbal explanations and encourage group discussions. Consider using recorded lectures or podcasts as supplemental learning resources to reinforce the material.
- **Read/write learners:** They prefer written texts and enjoy taking notes and writing summaries. To support read/write learners, provide well-structured handouts, textbooks, and reading materials. Please encourage them to create study guides, write reflections, and engage in written exercises to deepen their comprehension.
- **Kinesthetic learners:** Learners who thrive when engaged in hands-on experiences and physical activities. To cater to kinesthetic learners, incorporate interactive learning opportunities and practical exercises. Encourage movement during lessons and consider using props or real-life examples to make abstract concepts more tangible.

Now, let's explore how these learning styles vary across grade levels, from primary to high school. Younger students in primary grades typically exhibit more kinesthetic and visual learning tendencies. They learn best through play-based activities and experiential learning. As students' progress to secondary stages, auditory and read/write learning styles become more prominent. Finally, in high school, students often develop a balanced approach, incorporating multiple learning styles to adapt to various subjects and complexities.

To effectively teach different learners across grade levels, consider implementing the following strategies:

**Visual Learners**:

Primary Level (Grade 1-5):

- Use colorful charts, posters, and pictures to illustrate concepts.
- Incorporate educational videos or animations to reinforce learning.
- Organize field trips to museums or interactive exhibits to enhance visual learning.

Secondary Level (Grade 6-9):

- Use mind maps or concept maps to assist students in visualizing relationships between ideas.
- Create interactive presentations with visuals, such as Prezi or PowerPoint.

- Encourage students to design and showcase visual projects like posters or infographics.

High School Level (Grade 10-12):

- Use interactive whiteboards or online visual tools for demonstrations and explanations.
- Incorporate virtual reality (VR) experiences to immerse visual learners in various subjects.
- Organize classroom discussions with visual aids, like art pieces or historical photographs.

**Audio Learners**:

Primary Level (Grade 1-5):

- Use rhymes, songs, and chants to teach new concepts or reinforce information.
- Produce audio recordings of stories or readings for students to listen to.
- Conduct class discussions and debates to encourage verbal interactions.

Secondary Level (Grade 6-9):

- Incorporate educational podcasts or audiobooks for literature studies.
- Use speech-to-text technology to allow students to express ideas verbally.
- Encourage students to present their ideas through audio recordings or podcasts.

High School Level (Grade 10-12):

- Conduct role-playing exercises and simulations for historical or social studies lessons.
- Integrate audio-based quizzes or interactive voice response activities.
- Encourage students to participate in debates or deliver oral presentations fostering their motivation and active involvement.

**Read/Write Learners:**

Primary Level (Grade 1-5):

- Provide printed worksheets or writing exercises to reinforce learning.
- Encourage students to keep journals or write short stories about their experiences.
- Create reading circles where students can discuss books and written materials.

Secondary Level (Grade 6-9):

- Use interactive writing platforms to encourage collaborative writing among students.
- Incorporate book reviews and essay assignments to develop critical reading and writing skills.
- Encourage students to create blogs or online portfolios to showcase their work.

High School Level (Grades 10-12):

- Introduce research projects that require extensive reading and writing.
- Use online discussion forums or collaborative writing tools for group projects.
- Offer students chances to showcase their research findings through writing reports.

**Kinesthetic Learners**:

Primary Level (Grade 1-5):

- Engage in hands-on science experiments and nature exploration.
- Incorporate educational games and activities that involve physical movement, like scavenger hunts.
- Incorporate role-playing and dramatic activities to bring historical events to life.

Secondary Level (Grade 6-9):

- Integrate group projects that involve building physical models or prototypes.
- Incorporate physical games or simulations to teach mathematical concepts or problem-solving.
- Conduct hands-on art projects or crafts that align with subject matters.

High School Level (Grade 10-12):

- Introduce real-world simulations or business simulations for practical learning.
- Conduct interactive workshops or debates to encourage active participation.
- Organize field trips that offer hands-on experiences related to the curriculum.

Incorporate these practical strategies and deeply understand your student's unique learning styles. Foster a vibrant and inclusive learning environment that nurtures the full potential of each learner in your classroom. Remember that each student is different, so cater to their diverse needs to ignite a lifelong passion for learning.

## REMEMBER TO TAKE A BREAK!

Taking breaks is essential for students and teachers to maintain focus, improve productivity, and enhance overall well-being. Research has shown that regular intervals can significantly boost learning and cognitive abilities (Jagoo, 2021).

Studies have indicated that the brain functions in cycles of focus and rest. One notable research by DeskTime (2014), a productivity app, found that the most productive employees practiced the "52/17 Rule." This rule recommends concentrating intensely for 52 minutes, followed by a 17-minute break before resuming work. The results showed that those who followed this pattern exhibited higher productivity, maintaining their focus during work and recharging during breaks.

To implement the "52/17 Rule," follow these:

1. Set a timer or use a productivity app to work with total concentration for 52 minutes.
2. During the work session, stay focused and steer clear of distractions like social media or unrelated tasks.
3. Once the 52 minutes are up, take a 17-minute break.
4. Utilize the break to stretch, take a short walk, or engage in a relaxing activity to recharge your mind.

Another effective technique is the Pomodoro Technique, developed by Francesco Cirillo (Scroggs, n.d.). This approach entails breaking work into focused intervals, each followed by short breaks. Each work interval, commonly known as "Pomodoro," is typically 25 minutes long and followed by a 5-minute break. Following completing four Pomodoros, it is recommended to take a longer break lasting 15–30 minutes.

To implement the Pomodoro technique:

1. Set a timer or use a Pomodoro app to work for 25 minutes without interruptions.
2. After completing one Pomodoro, take a 5-minute break to rest and recharge.
3. Continue the process for four Pomodoros, then take a longer break. Lastly, incorporating brain breaks is essential for students to focus and retain information better (Morin, n.d.). Brain breaks are short, active breaks during learning sessions that allow students to refresh their minds and bodies. These breaks help

prevent burnout, increase attention spans, and improve classroom engagement.

To include brain breaks in the classroom:

1. Plan short, fun activities that involve physical movement or mental relaxation.
2. Integrate brain breaks strategically between longer learning sessions.
3. Encourage students to actively participate in the breaks, fostering a positive and energized atmosphere.

To sum up, taking regular breaks is not an indicator of laziness but rather an essential component of enhancing productivity and learning. Whether following the "52/17 Rule," implementing the Pomodoro Technique, or incorporating brain breaks, you and your students can reap the benefits of enhanced focus and improved retention.

## NAVIGATING CONVERSATIONS

Navigating conversations with students' parents is an integral part of a teacher's role, and it comes with its unique set of challenges. While our main focus is educating students, fostering a healthy and open relationship with parents is crucial in establishing a supportive learning environment. Yet, we must acknowledge that there are different types of parents, and it's inevitable to encounter difficult ones.

Dealing with challenging parents calls for caution, but approaching these conversations with empathy and a problem-solving mindset will likely yield positive outcomes. Remaining calm and composed during these interactions is one of the initial steps to take. Take a deep breath and uphold a professional demeanor to prevent tension from escalating. Practice actively listening to the parent's concerns without interruption, allowing them the opportunity to express themselves fully.

Finding common ground can be instrumental in building rapport and resolving issues. Look for areas of agreement with the parent to establish a positive foundation for communication. Validating their feelings and showing understanding will enable you to create an atmosphere of trust.

Setting clear boundaries and expectations for communication is crucial. Respectfully let parents know the best times and methods to reach you, ensuring you have designated moments for parent-teacher conferences or discussions.

Instead of focusing solely on problems, offer potential solutions and collaborate constructively with the parents to address their concerns. Engage in discussions about strategies to improve specific issues and collaborate to support the child's growth and development.

Keeping a record of your conversations with parents can be advantageous for future reference. Document the concerns raised, actions taken, and any agreed-upon solutions. This documentation can assist in maintaining continuity and progress in resolving issues.

If you come across an especially challenging situation, don't hesitate to seek out support from your colleagues, school administrators, or counseling resources. Having a support system can prove to be incredibly beneficial when it comes to navigating challenging conversations effectively.

After resolving an issue, follow up with the parents to ensure that progress is being made and that concerns have been addressed satisfactorily. This follow-up demonstrates your commitment to the student's well-being and academic success.

## Navigating the Classroom

| Questions | Sample Answer | Your Answer |
| --- | --- | --- |
| How do you currently assess the learning styles of your students? | I observe their preferences during class activities and use surveys to gather feedback. | |
| Can you provide an example of a lesson plan modification that successfully catered to various learning styles? | I incorporated group discussions, and visual aids. | |
| What adjustments can you make to your teaching approach to ensure inclusivity for all learners? | I plan to include more interactive elements and offer alternative materials for different learning preferences. | |
| How do you currently tailor your teaching strategies to different age groups? | I adapt complex content and use age-appropriate activities. | |
| What evidence-based practices can you incorporate to enhance knowledge retention? | I'm planning to integrate spaced repetition and active learning techniques based on recent research findings. | |

| | |
|---|---|
| **How can research findings on effective teaching strategies be applied across different age groups?** | Strategies like formative assessment can be adapted with age-appropriate materials and approaches. |
| **In what ways can incorporating regular breaks positively impact students' focus and well-being?** | Breaks allow students to recharge and reduce stress which helps maintain their concentration. |
| **Can you create a schedule template with break intervals and suggestions for rejuvenating activities?** | 52/17 rule: 52 minutes of focused work, followed by a 17-minute break. |
| **How do you currently approach communication with challenging parents?** | I emphasize active listening, empathy, and open-mindedness to build understanding and collaboration. |
| **What proactive steps can you take to address potential challenges in parent-teacher interactions?** | I plan to set clear expectations early in the year and maintain regular communication. |
| **Can you share a scenario of a challenging parent-teacher conversation and strategies to resolve it professionally?** | For example, if a parent is concerned about grading I schedule a meeting, share the grading criteria, and seek collaborative solutions. |

7

# REALIGNING PRIORITIES WITH GOAL SETTING

As educators, we often find ourselves on a quest to achieve success, striving to meet the expectations of others and fulfill predefined standards. What if success cannot be defined by a single universal approach? What if your definition of success is unique and doesn't align with societal norms or external pressures?

In this chapter, I invite you to embark on a reflective journey to uncover your definition of success. Let's explore what success means and how setting meaningful goals and recognizing priorities can lead you toward genuine fulfillment.

Before we delve into the practical aspects of goal setting, let's pause and reflect on your understanding of success. Pause and take a moment to reflect on your personal definition of success in your career as an educator. Is it reaching a particular milestone with your students? Is it fostering a love for learning in every child's heart? Or is it achieving a harmonious work-life balance that nurtures your own well-being?

In my early career, I pursued success in accounting, believing it was the key to achievement and fulfillment. I diligently chased after what I thought others deemed successful—promotions, accolades, and financial gains. Yet, as I neared these milestones, I felt anxious and stressed, questioning whether this version of success was meant for me.

In this moment of reflection, I realized I had been measuring success through the lens of external expectations rather than aligning it with my values and aspirations. I discovered that success lies in authenticity and defining my path rather than conforming to societal norms. This profound realization transformed my perspective, and I knew it was time to redefine my goals and priorities.

Defining success requires introspection and reflection on what truly brings joy and fulfillment in your role as a teacher. To do so, identify your passions and values, and set goals that align with your core beliefs. Embrace flexibility knowing success is a dynamic journey that evolves with time and circumstances.

Triumph encompasses more than just career achievements; it includes personal well-being, relationships, and hobbies. It's perfectly normal for your definition of success to evolve as you progress in your journey, which is completely acceptable. Trust your instincts, align your decisions with your values, and find contentment in your choices.

Knowing what success looks like helps realign priorities with goal setting. With a clear vision of your aspirations, you can set meaningful and authentic goals driven by your passion for teaching and desire to make a positive impact.

## SETTING YOUR GOALS

Goal setting provides us with the direction and purpose of our endeavors. When we have specific objectives, we become more focused and driven to achieve them. Research has shown that individuals who set clear goals are more likely to succeed and experience a sense of accomplishment (Locke & Latham, 2006). It's like having a roadmap guiding us toward our destination, ensuring we stay on track and progress.

In addition to providing direction, goal setting brings forth a multitude of advantages. By promoting greater efficiency and effectiveness, it enhances performance and productivity significantly. When we have a target, we better manage our time and resources. When we achieve our goal, it elevates our self-esteem and confidence, further strengthening our belief in our capabilities.

Moreover, setting and achieving goals can significantly impact our motivation. When we experience progress and success, our enthusiasm and drive increase. Each small win builds momentum, leading to greater accomplishments (Latham & Locke, 2007).

Goal setting also plays a crucial impact on mental well-being. Clearly defined goals alleviate stress and anxiety, providing a sense of control and purpose. When we know what we want to achieve and have a plan, we can better cope with challenges and uncertainties (Hollenbeck et al., 1989).

The effective establishment of goals is essential for attaining success and personal growth. Below are some tips and strategies to assist you in establishing goals that are both attainable and inspiring:

1. **Be specific:** Clearly articulate your goals and make them as precise as possible. As an example, rather than saying, "I want to improve as a teacher," articulate your goal as, "Incorporate interactive activities in the classroom to increase student engagement."
2. **Establish practical goals:** Make certain that your objectives can be accomplished within a reasonable timeframe. As an example, you can enhance achievability by breaking down larger objectives into smaller, manageable steps.
3. **Develop a timeline:** Assign deadlines to each goal to instill a sense of urgency and accountability. A timeline will keep you on track and help you measure your progress.
4. **Please write it down:** Document your goals on paper or a digital platform. Writing them down reinforces your commitment and helps you focus on your goals.
5. **Maintain a positive outlook:** Sustain a positive mindset and visualize the successful realization of your goals. Optimistic thinking can boost you and heighten

your motivation and confidence, thereby facilitating the process of overcoming challenges.

For instance, teachers endeavor to incorporate more hands-on activities in their science lessons. They define this goal specifically by including interactive experiments once a week. Since they have other responsibilities, they start with one weekly experiment and gradually increase the frequency.

Recognizing and celebrating each success, big or small, is a crucial aspect of goal setting. Celebrating achievements provides positive reinforcement, boosts motivation, and builds self-confidence. By acknowledging progress and accomplishments, educators create a sense of fulfillment and satisfaction, encouraging them to continue working towards future goals.

For example, after implementing the first interactive science experiment in their class, a teacher takes a moment to acknowledge their efforts and celebrates the engaged responses from their students. This positive experience motivates them to plan the next experiment. This reinforces their conviction in the efficacy of hands-on activities for enhancing their students' learning.

## LITTLE WINS MATTER TOO

In pursuing our goals, we must recognize that little wins matter too. Celebrating these small victories can bring a sense of internal satisfaction and pride, which plays a significant role in motivating us to strive for more significant achievements.

Our brains are wired with a negativity bias, meaning we tend to focus more on our failures and shortcomings than our successes. This natural inclination can lead to discouragement and self-doubt, making staying motivated in the face of challenges challenging. However, celebrating small wins can help counter this bias and shift our focus toward the positive aspects of our journey.

Celebrating the achievement of small, intermediate goals sends positive signals to our brain, triggering the release of dopamine —the feel-good chemical associated with pleasure and reward. This surge of dopamine reinforces the neural pathways associated with the actions that led to the accomplishment, making it more likely for us to repeat those actions in the future.

For example, a teacher aims to improve classroom management by implementing a behavior reward system. Each time a student follows the rules or demonstrates positive behavior, the teacher acknowledges their efforts and rewards them with praise or a small token of recognition. This consistent celebration of small wins creates a positive classroom environment. It reinforces the desired behaviors, encouraging students to continue their good behavior.

Moreover, celebrating small wins provides a sense of progress and achievement, even when the larger goal might still feel distant. It enables us to divide complex tasks into manageable steps and recognize our progress. As we see ourselves making incremental progress, we gain confidence in our abilities and feel more motivated to tackle the challenges.

By welcoming the value of little wins, we create a positive feedback loop that propels us forward, increasing our motivation and resilience. These celebratory moments fuel our determination, serving as a reminder that every small step forward brings us closer to our bigger goals.

As we've explored in this chapter, defining success on your terms and aligning your priorities can be transformative. Now, it's time to put that knowledge into action and create a concrete plan to achieve the goals that will lead you to your version of success.

Begin by visualizing your goals and aspirations. What are your aspirations for the upcoming days, months, and even years? Pause and contemplate what truly holds significance to you and consider the steps you can take to reach those goals.

To help you get started, I've prepared a sample goal action plan that you can use as a guide. This action plan will assist you in mapping out your objectives, setting deadlines, and identifying the strategies you'll employ to achieve your dreams.

**Sample Goal Action Plan:**

**Goal:** [Clearly state your goal here]

**Start Date**: [Specify when you'll begin working towards this goal]

---

**Target Date:** [Establish a practical deadline for accomplishing your goal]

---

**Solution:** [Outline the steps and strategies you'll use to achieve the goal]

---

---

---

---

**Status Update**: [Monitor the progress you have made so far in pursuit of your goal]

---

---

---

---

**Contemplation**: Pause and on your journey. What aspects of pursuing this goal have you found easy and enjoyable? During your journey, what challenges have you encountered? How have you overcome those challenges or plan to address them moving forward?

---

---

---

---

Remember, this action plan is a flexible tool. As you progress, adjust it according to your needs and experiences. Be kind to yourself and embrace the process of growth and learning. Celebrate each little win and use the strategies you've discovered in this chapter to keep yourself motivated and focused.

## Realigning Priorities With Goal Setting

| Questions | Sample Answer | Your Answer |
| --- | --- | --- |
| **What does success mean to you personally, and how does it align with your values and aspirations?** | Success to me means achieving a balance between personal fulfillment, meaningful relationships, and personal growth. | |
| **How can acknowledging the uniqueness of your definition of success impact your goal-setting journey?** | Understanding my unique definition helps me set authentic and meaningful goals that align with my values. | |
| **Can you share stories of individuals redefining success on their terms and finding fulfillment?** | An entrepreneur who prioritizes work-life balance over traditional markers of success. | |

| | |
|---|---|
| **How do your current priorities align with your long-term aspirations, and how can setting specific goals help you progress in those areas?** | At the moment, my priorities are my career advancement and personal development. |
| **Can you offer a personalized guide on setting SMART goals tailored to your individual needs?** | Define clear goals, establish criteria that are quantifiable, ensure realistic goals that align with my aspirations, and set deadlines for them. |
| **How does achieving goals positively impact confidence and well-being, and why is the journey as valuable as the result?** | Achieving goals boosts confidence and the journey provides opportunities to grow. |
| **In what ways does recognizing and celebrating progress aid in sustaining a positive mindset during challenging times?** | Recognizing and celebrating progress increases resilience and motivation. |
| **Offer creative ways to celebrate small victories along the goal-setting journey.** | A great way to celebrate small victories is to share your achievements with friends and family. Alternatively, you can create a progress journal. |
| **How can you perceive challenges and setbacks as chances for growth and development in pursuit of your goals?** | Challenges provide opportunities to grow, to adapt, and to shape my character. |
| **Share personal experiences of individuals using setbacks as chances for growth.** | When athletes face injuries and they see it as a chance to improve their mental and physical resilience. |
| **How can you review and customize the sample goal action plan to make it more effective for your specific ambitions?** | You can do this by reviewing each step and changing it to match your timeline and suit your unique circumstances. |

# 8

## HEALTH CLASS IN PROGRESS

Teaching is a dignified and rewarding profession, but it can also be physically demanding. The long hours on our feet, constantly moving around the classroom, bending and stretching to engage our students—no wonder teaching feels like an all-day cardio workout! But let's not forget the countless sleepless nights spent grading papers, preparing lessons, and worrying about our students' success. The mental and emotional energy we invest in is immeasurable and affects our well-being.

I was once caught up in the whirlwind of teaching, fueled by an unwavering desire to give my best to my students. Yet, I failed to realize that neglecting my health was doing me more harm than good. I often forgo proper sleep to finish grading assignments or wake up early to prepare elaborate lesson plans. My meals consisted of quick snacks grabbed between classes or forgotten altogether in the hustle and bustle of the school day. And don't even get me started on the lack of movement—I spent hours on end glued to my desk.

Before long, I found myself experiencing burnout. My energy levels plummeted, and my motivation waned. I became irritable, and my passion for teaching seemed to fade away. It was a wake-up call that taught me a valuable lesson—I needed to prioritize my physical and mental well-being to be an effective teacher.

Our health is not a compartmentalized aspect of our lives; it's interconnected. When we neglect one area, it affects others too. A lack of sleep can increase stress levels and weaken immunity, making us more susceptible to illnesses. Unhealthy eating habits can zap our energy and hinder our ability to focus and make sound decisions in the classroom. Minimal physical activity can lead to physical ailments and mental fatigue, hindering our enthusiasm for teaching.

This chapter explores practical tips and advice to help you create a sustainable routine that prioritizes your health. We'll cover everything from sleep and nutrition to movement and self-care.

As teachers, we have the privilege and responsibility of shaping young minds. But to do so effectively and with passion, we must first care for ourselves.

## DON'T FORGET TO...

The link between physical health and mental health is intricate and profound. As educators, we must recognize how they intertwine and impact each other. Scientific research has shown that mental health issues can significantly affect one's physical health, just as one's physical health can profoundly influence their mental well-being.

Multiple studies have established the link between mental and physical health, unveiling how stress, anxiety, and depression can have physical manifestations. Chronic stress, for instance, can lead to increased cortisol levels in the body, which may contribute to weight gain, sleep disturbances, and immune system suppression (Yaribeygi et al., 2017). Similarly, anxiety and depression have been associated with cardiovascular problems, such as hypertension and heart disease (Katon et al., 2007).

On the other hand, our physical health also plays a vital role in impacting our mental well-being. Regular physical activity, such as exercise, has been linked to improved mood and reduced symptoms of anxiety and depression (Yaribeygi et al., 2017). Exercise releases endorphins, commonly known as "feel-good" hormones, which can lift our spirits and enhance our overall well-being.

With the demands of a teacher's busy schedule, finding time to prioritize our health can seem impossible. The relentless cycle of lesson planning, grading, meetings, and extracurricular activities leaves little room for self-care.

Nevertheless, this aspect gently reminds us that self-care is not a luxury but an essential necessity. It's essential to recognize that when we neglect our physical and mental health, we compromise our ability to be effective educators. Teaching is an emotionally and physically demanding profession, and we owe it to ourselves and our students to be in the best possible shape.

The following pages explore practical strategies and tips to incorporate self-care into our busy lives. Caring for ourselves is not selfish; it's an investment in our well-being.

EAT

Teachers play an indispensable role in influencing their students' eating habits and health-related behaviors. As the saying goes, "actions speak louder than words," and this couldn't be truer when it comes to a teacher's impact on their students' dietary intake. Research has shown that teachers are important role models for students, influencing their food choices and health behaviors inside and outside the classroom (Parker et al., 2020).

Over the past years, numerous schools have introduced policies and programs to tackle childhood obesity and encourage healthier eating habits among students. However, giving equal consideration to the nutrition-related practices of teachers themselves is of paramount importance. A study evaluated obesity-related health behaviors among teachers and found that teachers' diet quality was associated with their nutrition-related practices in the classroom (Folta et al., 2020). When teachers demonstrated healthy eating behaviors, such as consuming fruits and vegetables or drinking water in front of their students, it positively impacted their dietary choices.

As teachers spend substantial time with their students during the school day, they have abundant opportunities to exemplify healthy eating behaviors and integrate nutrition knowledge into their daily classroom activities. This way, we encourage our students to adopt similar healthy habits, improving overall dietary intake and health-related outcomes (Parker et al., 2020).

Furthermore, avoiding unhealthy food practices, such as food rewards or food-based celebrations, can contribute to a positive school food environment. Teachers should be attentive to the types of foods they introduce to their students and cultivate a supportive atmosphere that promotes healthy eating choices.

I personally struggled to find time for healthy meals during the school day. However, I started planning my lunches ahead of time and packing them in containers. As an example, On Sundays, I would prepare a batch of vibrant salads containing protein-rich ingredients such as grilled chicken or chickpeas. Throughout the week, I had nutritious and delicious lunches ready to go, helping me resist the temptation of unhealthy fast food.

Additionally, I stocked my desk with nutritious snacks like almonds, yogurt, and fresh fruit. When I felt hungry between classes, I reached for these healthier options instead of vending machine snacks. These small changes in my eating habits significantly impacted my energy levels and overall well-being throughout the school day.

Allow me to share with you some of the keys I learned during this process to improve my eating habits:

- **Engage in meal planning and preparation ahead of time:** Allocate some time, during the weekend to plan your meals for the week ahead. Create a shopping list and buy healthy ingredients in advance. Preparing nutritious meals in batches and storing them in containers can save you time during busy weekdays. For example, you can make a large pot of vegetable soup and portion it out for quick lunches throughout the week.

- **Maintain a supply of healthy snacks on hand:** Keep nuts, fruits, granola bars, or yogurt cups readily available in your desk or bag. Making healthy options readily available decreases the probability of resorting to unhealthy alternatives when hunger strikes. For instance, keep a bag of mixed nuts in your desk drawer for a satisfying and nourishing mid-afternoon snack.

- **Adopt mindful eating habits:** Practice alternative eating by paying close attention to your body's hunger and fullness cues. Refrain from eating at your desk or while multitasking. Instead, take a break and enjoy your meal without distractions. For instance, step away from your work area when you have lunch, sit down, and focus on your meal.

- **Opt for balanced meals:** Include protein, healthy fats, complex carbohydrates, and vegetables in your diet. A simple plate could consist of grilled chicken, quinoa, roasted vegetables, and a small side of avocado. This combination provides essential sustenance to maintain your energy levels throughout the day.

- **Hydration is key:** Keep a reusable water bottle and habitually sip water throughout the day. Ensuring proper hydration is vital for sustaining energy levels and overall well-being. As a teacher, you can set a good example by having a water bottle on your desk and encouraging your students to do the same.

- **Reduce sugary beverage intake:** Limit the consumption of sugary drinks like soda and fruit juices that contain high levels of sugar. Instead, choose water, herbal tea, or naturally flavored water with fresh fruits or herbs. You can infuse a pitcher of water with cucumber and mint for a refreshing, sugar-free alternative.
- **Practice mindful indulgence:** It's okay to indulge in your favorite treats occasionally but do so mindfully. Delight in the taste and relish the experience without any sense of guilt. Remember, moderation is the key to maintaining a healthy relationship with food.

Taking care of your health might appear overwhelming, particularly with a busy teacher's schedule. Incremental actions over time lead to significant improvements. Start by incorporating one healthy eating habit at a time, such as packing a nutritious lunch or choosing healthier snacks. As you build up slowly, you'll find that these changes become more manageable and sustainable.

MOVE

Exercise offers benefits beyond physical health; it can also boost your performance as a teacher. Scientific research shows regular exercise can boost cognitive function, memory, and overall mood (Hillman et al., 2008; Loprinzi et al., 2020). As you exercise, your brain releases neurotransmitters like dopamine and endorphins, responsible for feelings of happiness and reduced stress (Hillman et al., 2008). This improved mental state can positively influence your teaching abilities and student interactions.

Despite a demanding schedule, finding time to exercise is essential for your well-being. Presented below are six practical tips to assist you in integrating physical activity into your daily routine:

- **Begin with the day with invigorating morning walks:** Set aside 20 minutes for a brisk walk before school starts. It will invigorate your mind and set a positive tone for the day. • Active breaks: Use short breaks during the school day to stretch, do some jumping jacks, or take a quick stroll around the classroom. These brief bursts of activity can accumulate and create a significant impact over time.
- **Incorporate lunchtime workouts:** Make use of your lunch break for a swift workout session. Whether it's a short jog, yoga session, or bodyweight exercises, you'll feel more energized and focused in the afternoon.
- **Involve students:** Incorporate movement into your lessons by encouraging students to stand up and participate in physical activities. Not only will they benefit, but you'll also feel more engaged and motivated.
- **Group activities:** Connect with fellow teachers for after-school group workouts or sports. Exercising together can be fun and provide social support.
- **Home workouts:** On days when going to the gym is challenging, follow online workout videos or use fitness apps to exercise at home. This choice offers both convenience and flexibility. You don't need to become a weightlifter or spend hours at the gym to reap the benefits of exercise. Aim for 30 minutes of moderate-intensity exercise three to four times a week, and you'll notice positive changes in your physical and mental well-

being (U.S. Department of Health and Human Services, 2018).

Consistency is vital; over time, these small efforts will contribute to a healthier, happier you.

## REST

Restful sleep is a cornerstone of a healthy lifestyle, especially for teachers facing the demands of their profession. Thus, how much sleep do you require? Experts recommend that adults aim for 7–9 hours of sleep each night (Suni & Singh, 2023). Nonetheless, individual requirements may differ, so it is crucial to listen to your body and ensure you feel refreshed and rejuvenated.

Insufficient sleep can have a negative impact on both your physical and mental well-being. Lack of sleep can lead to decreased cognitive function, reduced focus and attention, impaired memory, and increased irritability (Alhola & Polo-Kantola, 2007). In the classroom setting, inadequate sleep may impact your ability to engage students effectively, impacting both your teaching and their learning experiences.

Practicing healthy sleep hygiene is essential to get the rest you need. Below are some practical tips to enhance the quality of your sleep, even with a busy schedule:

- **Establish a bedtime routine:** Create a calming pre-sleep ritual to signal your body that it is time to unwind and prepare for rest. Participating in activities like reading a book, meditating, and taking a warm bath can be calming and soothing.

- **Reduce screen time:** Limit your exposure to screens (phone, TV, computer) at least an hour before bedtime. The blue light emitted from screens can disturb your sleep-wake cycle.
- **Keep a consistent sleep schedule:** Strive to go to bed and wake up at the same times every day, including weekends. Having a consistent sleep schedule aids in regulating your body's internal clock.
- **Establish a sleep-friendly environment:** Maintain a cool, dark, and quiet bedroom setting to encourage better sleep. Consider investing in cozy bedding and a mattress that provides excellent support.
- **Limit your intake of caffeine and alcohol:** Avoid consuming these substances near bedtime, as they can interfere with the quality of your sleep
- **Control daytime naps:** While short power naps can be rejuvenating, avoid long ones that might interfere with your nighttime sleep.

Here's an example of applying these tips: Establish a bedtime routine by setting aside 30 minutes before bedtime to read a book or practice gentle stretches. Dim the lights in your bedroom and silence your phone to create a calming environment. You will discover that this routine helps you unwind and prepares you for a peaceful night's sleep.

Practicing healthy eating habits, regular exercise, and prioritizing sleep go hand in hand with overall well-being. When you take care of your physical health, your body and mind are better equipped to handle the challenges of teaching. A balanced approach to health will help you maintain the energy and focus needed to be your best teacher.

## Health Class in Progress

| Questions | Sample Answer | Your Answer |
| --- | --- | --- |
| How can you identify signs of stress in your teaching routine, and what self-awareness strategies can you employ? | Some of the signs may include lack of focus, irritability, or fatigue. A common strategy to deal with it involves self-check-ins and mindfulness practices. | |
| How do healthy eating habits contribute to your overall well-being as an educator? | Good nutrition provides the energy and mental clarity to support your overall health. | |
| In what ways does regular exercise positively impact your performance in the classroom? | It can boost performance in the classroom by increasing energy levels and reducing stress, which often leads to more effective teaching. | |
| How does sufficient rest play a pivotal role in maintaining your physical and mental health? | Sufficient rest helps with immune function, cognitive abilities, and mood regulation,which are essential for effective teaching. | |
| Why is tracking your habits essential for maintaining a healthy lifestyle as a teacher? | This is true because tracking habits creates awareness, which helps identify patterns and helps with motivation. | |

| | |
|---|---|
| **Share a specific habit-tracking strategy that has worked for you in the past.** | You can use an app to track your habits or a journal to check on your daily exercises, nutrition, and sleep. |
| **How do you plan to incorporate the key takeaways into your teaching routine moving forward?** | By scheduling regular breaks and maintaining a balanced diet. |

# 9
# BUILDING YOUR SUPPORT SYSTEM



*"If you want to go quickly, go alone. If you want to go far, go together."*

— *AFRICAN PROVERB*

In this chapter, we embark on a journey that explores the immense significance of community in our lives as teachers. As educators, we often find ourselves engrossed in the demanding teaching world, focusing on nurturing young minds and shaping the future. However, we must recognize that our well-being and personal growth are also deeply intertwined with the connections we build and foster within our community.

Community plays a multifaceted role in our lives, impacting our emotional and spiritual health and presenting avenues for professional advancement. Through this exploration, we will uncover the profound impact of meaningful relationships on our overall well-being and how they can serve as a source of support and inspiration amidst our busy schedules.

Join me as we explore the art of creating and maintaining connections that can enrich our lives as teachers, enhance our teaching experience, and ultimately contribute to our success and fulfillment as educators.

## THE IMPORTANCE OF COMMUNITY

In the stir and clamor of our lives as teachers, we often seek refuge and solace in the sense of belonging we find within our community. But what does a sense of belonging truly mean? It is that warm feeling of being accepted, valued, and connected to like-minded individuals who share common goals, interests, and experiences. In these moments, we realize we are not alone in our journey as educators and that we can overcome challenges and celebrate triumphs together.

Imagine the camaraderie of a teacher's lounge, where colleagues exchange stories, laughter, and advice, creating an atmosphere of support and understanding. Or picture yourself in a virtual educator's network, where you can share innovative teaching techniques and receive inspiration from educators worldwide. These are real-life examples of a sense of belonging in action, where teachers unite, building a community that thrives on collaboration and sharing the passion for education.

The impact of a sense of belonging is profound and far-reaching. Studies have shown that individuals who feel connected to their community experience increased happiness levels, reduced stress and anxiety, and improved overall well-being. This feeling of belonging serves as a safety net, offering emotional support and encouragement during difficult times. It enhances our resilience, empowering us to weather the storms that may arise in our teaching careers.

Beyond personal well-being, being part of an engaging community also offers tremendous benefits in our professional lives. In a community, we realize the strength of collaboration, understanding that our abilities may complement someone else's weaknesses and vice versa. By embracing this synergy, we create an environment where ideas are freely exchanged, expertise is shared, and creativity is nurtured. The collective knowledge and experience of the community enrich each teacher's pedagogy and elevates the teaching profession as a whole.

As teachers, we are part of a unique tribe with a shared purpose —to ignite a passion for learning within our students and shape future generations. In this shared journey, we find comfort and inspiration in the hearts and minds of our fellow educators. The significance of community in our lives cannot be emphasized enough. The heartbeat sustains, empowers, and propels us toward greater personal and professional growth. Let us embrace the power of belonging, as together, we thrive and flourish in the transformative world of education.

## EXPANDING YOUR CIRCLES AND YOUR CAREER

One way to foster a sense of belonging is by exploring various types of communities. Neighbors can provide a local support system, faith-based organizations offer spiritual connection, and hobby-focused clubs unite individuals with shared interests. Volunteer groups allow us to give back to society, while alum networks reunite us with past connections. Coworking spaces can cultivate collaboration, while professional development groups provide chances for skill enhancement. Lastly, employee resource groups create inclusive workplaces that cater to diverse identities and experiences (Wooll, 2021).

To find our communities, we can follow several effective tips. Firstly, consider seeking local groups that align with our passions or interests. For example, joining national or state-level organizations for teachers can provide a platform for networking and staying updated on educational trends. Attending conferences and workshops on classroom management and student engagement enhances knowledge and opens doors to meeting like-minded educators. Engaging in mentorship programs or peer-mentoring opportunities nurtures valuable relationships that can shape our careers.

Moreover, investing in our personal development through certifications, workshops, and online courses strengthens our expertise. It connects us with individuals sharing similar professional aspirations. Engaging in advanced education, like pursuing a master's degree, can broaden our academic and social circles. Engaging in volunteer and service activities enables us to connect with the community and create a positive impact.

While actively seeking community involvement is beneficial, it is also essential to strike a balance and set boundaries. As educators, our time holds great value, and managing personal and professional obligations can be demanding. Finding our communities inside and outside Work creates a sense of belonging that strengthens our emotional and spiritual health. Expanding our circles through professional development and networking enriches our careers and allows us to learn from others' experiences. In pursuing community, let us remember the value of boundaries, ensuring that our relationships and well-being thrive harmoniously.

## BOUNDARIES

Boundaries are essential guidelines that define the limits of acceptable behavior, both for us and in our interactions with others. They serve as the invisible line that protects our well-being and helps maintain healthy relationships. Healthy limits are crucial because they enable us to establish safety, respect, and balance in our personal and professional lives.

There are different types of limitations that we can establish in various aspects of our lives:

- **Physical boundaries** establish our personal space and the extent of physical contact we find comfortable. For example, expressing the need for personal space when someone stands too close or saying no to physical touch makes us uncomfortable.

- **Emotional boundaries:** They protect our feelings and emotions. It involves recognizing and communicating our feelings and needs while also respecting the feelings of others. For instance, setting limits on sharing personal information or not allowing others to manipulate our emotions.
- **Professional boundaries:** Professional boundaries help us distinguish between personal and professional lives. This could involve not discussing personal issues with students or colleagues or not engaging in personal relationships with students.
- **Time boundaries:** These involve limiting the time and energy we dedicate to work, social activities, and personal pursuits. For instance, saying no to additional work tasks when overwhelmed or allocating specific time for self-care activities.
- **Material boundaries:** These are related to possessions and resources. It involves being assertive about our possessions and not allowing others to take advantage of our belongings without permission.
- **Digital boundaries:** With the prevalence of technology, digital boundaries are becoming increasingly important. This could include limiting screen time, managing social media usage, and protecting our personal information online.

Setting healthy boundaries is essential for our well-being because it helps us protect our mental and emotional health, prevents burnout, and fosters healthy relationships with others.

## AT WORK

Establishing workplace boundaries is crucial for upholding a healthy and productive work environment. Here are some principles for setting boundaries and practical examples to put them into practice:

- **Recognize your boundaries:** Take time to contemplate what situations make you feel uncomfortable or overwhelmed at Work. For example, suppose additional tasks beyond your capacity lead to stress and burnout. If that is the case, it's time to set limits on how much you can handle.
- **Practice clear and respectful communication:** When establishing boundaries, express your needs and limits clearly and assertively. For instance, kindly inform your colleagues if you prefer not to be disturbed during specific work hours.
- **Maintain consistency:** Consistency is crucial for establishing and upholding boundaries. If you have set specific working hours, adhere to them consistently to avoid confusion.
- **Developing the skill of saying no:** Learning to say no is essential for establishing boundaries. For example, politely decline and explain your reasons if you're asked to work late when it conflicts with your personal commitments.

- **Prioritize self-care:** Prioritize self-care and set aside time for rest and relaxation. For example, make it a priority to take regular breaks during work hours to recharge and prevent burnout.
- **Seek support:** If you encounter difficulty in setting boundaries, do not hesitate to reach out to your colleagues or supervisors for assistance. Share your concerns and ask for their understanding and support.

When someone breaks your boundary at Work, addressing the situation promptly and assertively is essential. Politely remind the person of your set boundary and express how their actions affect you. If the behavior continues, consider having a private conversation with the person to discuss the issue more in-depth.

When everyone in the workplace sets and respects boundaries, it fosters a positive and harmonious work environment. People feel respected and valued, leading to improved job satisfaction and productivity. Additionally, healthy boundaries encourage open communication and collaboration among colleagues, which enhances teamwork and creativity.

OUTSIDE WORK

Setting and maintaining good boundaries outside of Work is crucial for protecting your emotional and spiritual well-being and maintaining healthy relationships. Here are some tips on how to set and maintain boundaries in your personal life, along with real-life examples of how to put them into practice:

- **Understand your values and priorities:** Allocate some time to introspect on your values and what holds the greatest significance to you. This will aid you in establishing the boundaries you wish to set in various areas of your life. For instance, if spending quality time with family is a top priority, you can set boundaries around work commitments to ensure you have time for your loved ones.
- **Be explicit and assertive:** Clearly and confidently communicate your boundaries with others. For example, if you need time to recharge after a busy day, kindly express this to your friends or family without feeling guilty.
- **Create personal time and space:** Carve out personal time and space for activities that bring you joy and fulfillment. Whether pursuing a hobby, reading a book, or simply enjoying nature, this time allows you to recharge and connect with yourself.

You might be pondering how and in which situations to put these ideas into practice. Allow me to present you with some typical scenarios.

Imagine you have a family member who frequently drops by your home unannounced, disrupting your personal time and causing stress. Engage in an open and honest conversation with them to set a boundary. Express your need for some alone time and kindly ask them to call or message before coming over.

In a romantic relationship, setting boundaries can foster mutual understanding and respect. As an example, if you highly value your personal space and independence, you can communicate with your partner and let them know that you occasionally need time alone to recharge. This way, you avoid potential conflicts and reassure your partner that your boundaries do not reflect their value to you.

Suppose you have a friend who often asks for favors at inconvenient times, making it challenging for you to manage your responsibilities. Setting a boundary can be as simple as letting them know when you can help and when it's impossible. This subtle demeanor will maintain the friendship while ensuring that you prioritize your well-being and commitments.

Finally, in various social settings or professional environments, people may approach you with requests or demands beyond your capacity or comfort level. Setting boundaries with others involves being assertive and honest about your limitations. For example, suppose a colleague asks you to take on additional tasks. In that case, you can express that you have other commitments and suggest finding a more suitable solution together.

Recognizing that boundaries are not about building walls or shutting people out is important. Instead, they serve as protective fences that allow healthy and balanced relationships to thrive. As you grow more at ease with setting boundaries, you'll notice an enhancement in your overall well-being improves, and your relationships become more genuine and gratifying.

# Building Your Support System

| Questions | Sample Answer | Your Answer |
|---|---|---|
| How has being part of a supportive community influenced your emotional well-being and professional development? | Being part of a teaching community provides me with emotional support during challenging times, as well as opportunities for collaboration within my field. | |
| How can connecting with like-minded individuals enhance your sense of belonging and advance your career? | Connecting with other educators can lead to valuable insights, shared resources, and enhanced professional growth. | |
| How does a sense of belonging contribute to your overall well-being and happiness? | A sense of belonging brings a sense of purpose and reduces stress, which in turn contributes to overall life satisfaction and well-being. | |
| In what ways can active participation in engaging communities positively impact your personal and professional life? | Active participation helps with networking and develops a supportive environment for personal and career development. | |
| How can expanding your social circles contribute to a richer support system? | A diversified social circle provides different perspectives as well as opportunities for personal and professional growth. | |
| Offer networking strategies and tips for connecting with new people within your professional field. | You can attend industry events or sign up for online forums, as well as start conversations with colleagues in the same field. | |
| How can setting and respecting boundaries lead to more fulfilling relationships? | Setting boundaries provides a healthy balance and prevents burnout. | |

# 10

# MENTAL HEALTH BREAK

*"We continue progressing, unlocking fresh opportunities and exploring novel experiences because of our curiosity. And it is this curiosity that keeps guiding us along new paths."*

— *WALT DISNEY*

As we reach the final chapter of this journey together, I want to remind you of the importance of taking a step back, allowing yourself to breathe, and indulging in activities that bring out the inner child within you. In this last chapter, we will explore the wonders of curiosity and play and how they can significantly impact your mental health and overall well-being, regardless of age.

Like many of you, I once found myself caught in the whirlwind of the teaching profession, constantly juggling responsibilities and giving my all to ensure my students received the best education possible. I was determined to be the best teacher I could be, but somewhere along the way, I began to neglect an essential aspect of my growth—my mental health.

One day, feeling particularly overwhelmed and exhausted, I stumbled upon a forgotten hobby I had once enjoyed: painting. At that moment, I decided to pick up the paintbrush again and immerse myself in colors and creativity. As the paint flowed across the canvas, I felt a sense of tranquility and joy I hadn't experienced in a long time. It was as if I had reconnected with a part of myself that had been buried beneath the responsibilities of adulthood.

That simple act of engaging in a playful and creative activity helped me de-stress and sharpen my focus. When the new week began, I felt revitalized and more equipped to tackle the challenges ahead. I realized that taking breaks and nurturing my passions weren't selfish acts; instead, they were the key to improving my mental health and ultimately making me a better educator.

This chapter will dig deeper into the transformative power of curiosity and play. We'll explore how indulging in hobbies, engaging in playful activities, and embracing your inner child can elevate your well-being and foster a renewed enthusiasm for teaching.

As we approach the culmination of this book, I encourage you to rediscover the joy of curiosity, embrace the magic of play, and prioritize your mental health.

## HAVE YOU TAKEN A BREAK LATELY?

The profound impact of pleasurable leisure activities on general well-being and stress reduction is valuable. This is according to a study conducted by Pressman et al. in 2019. The study reveals an intriguing connection between engaging in more frequent enjoyable leisure activities and experiencing better psychological and physical well-being. Participants who actively embraced various pleasurable activities reported higher life satisfaction, life engagement, social support, and physical activity. Simultaneously, they encountered reduced levels of depression and negative emotions. Moreover, they exhibited better physical health indicators, such as lower blood pressure, cortisol levels, body mass index (BMI), and waist circumference (WC). Even after adjusting for demographic variables, this positive association remained evident.

These leisure activities encompass various pleasurable pursuits that individuals voluntarily engage in when they have free time, unrestricted by work or other responsibilities. From engaging in hobbies to social interactions and spending time in nature, these activities serve as vital "breathers" and "restorers," offering individuals a chance to take a break, immerse in enjoyable diversions, and subsequently experience positive emotions while reducing stress.

Moreover, the research explores how engaging in enjoyable leisure activities can buffer the negative psychological effects of stress. Participants who had faced higher stress levels due to past life events and engaged in more pleasurable leisure activities displayed lower negative moods and depression. Conversely, they exhibited higher levels of positive affect, life satisfaction, and engagement. These findings highlight the vital role of enjoyable leisure activities in providing a much-needed respite from stress, leading to enhanced restoration and resilience.

Considering the invaluable insights from this study, it becomes evident that leisure activities, such as vacations, hobbies, and self-care pursuits like spending time in nature, profoundly influence our mental health. Engaging in such activities fosters positive emotions, encourages social interactions, and promotes relaxation, all contributing to improved overall well-being and a better ability to cope with stress.

As educators, we often find ourselves consumed by the demanding nature of our profession, leaving little time for personal indulgences and leisure. However, this research reminds us to prioritize leisure and embrace activities that bring joy and relaxation. Whether it's taking a well-deserved vacation to recharge, dedicating time to hobbies that ignite our passions, or simply immersing ourselves in the serenity of nature, embracing leisure as an integral part of our lives can invigorate us with the energy, we need to approach our work with renewed vigor and enthusiasm.

## MAKING A SELF-CARE ROUTINE

Emphasizing the significance of a self-care routine is paramount in striving for a healthier and more rewarding teaching career. At its essence, a self-care plan acts as a tailor-made guide, empowering educators to prioritize their physical, emotional, and mental well-being through purposeful and deliberate practices. It underscores the notion that investing time in self-nurturing is not a mere indulgence but a vital requirement for fostering a harmonious work-life equilibrium.

The key aspects of a self-care plan encompass various dimensions of our well-being, and each aspect plays a vital role in our holistic development. Let's explore these aspects through relatable examples from the experiences shared in the previous chapters:

- **In terms of physical well-being:** This entails taking care of our bodies through regular exercise, maintaining nutritious eating habits, and ensuring sufficient rest. For instance, incorporating a morning yoga routine, like the one described in Chapter 8, will promote physical health and positively impact our mental and emotional state.
- **Emotionally:** Understanding and processing our emotions is crucial. Activities like journaling—as discussed in Chapter 3—helps release pent-up emotions and foster emotional clarity and self-awareness.
- **Mentally:** Our minds need stimulation and relaxation. Engaging in hobbies allows us to immerse ourselves in creative pursuits and alleviate mental fatigue.
- **Regarding social well-being:** Establishing and sustaining meaningful connections with others is essential for our social health. As exemplified in Chapter 9, joining a community or professional organization will offer support and camaraderie in both personal and career growth.

- **Spiritually:** This aspect is unique to each individual and can encompass activities that bring a sense of purpose and inner peace. As highlighted in the previous section, spending time in nature can be a soul-soothing experience.

Crafting a self-care plan involves five crucial steps:

- **Evaluation:** Take a moment to contemplate your present state of well-being and recognize any areas that need more focus and attention. For instance, drawing from the personal story in the chapter hook, a teacher may realize the need to prioritize sleep and emotional self-care.
- **Goal setting:** Establish realistic and achievable self-care goals. These could range from incorporating regular exercise, as inspired by Chapter 8, to engaging in regular creative outlets like photography or writing.
- **Creating a plan:** Devise a detailed plan that outlines specific self-care activities and how often you will engage in them. A teacher might allocate time for daily meditation, weekly walks in nature, and monthly outings with friends or family.
- **Embracing flexibility and adaptability:** Recognize that life can be unpredictable, and being open to adjustments may become necessary. Learn to adapt your self-care plan without judgment or guilt. Flexibility lets you stay committed to your overall well-being, as highlighted in the previous chapters' anecdotes.

When you prioritize your well-being, you enhance the quality of your life and elevate the standard of your work and your impact on your students. Nurture your physical, emotional, and mental health, and you will become a role model for your students, teaching them the importance of self-care and resilience. A thriving and balanced teacher will inspire a classroom filled with thriving and motivated learners.

## DON'T FORGET TO HAVE FUN

In my journey of self-discovery through a well-crafted self-care routine, I stumbled upon various hobbies like gardening and crocheting. These activities brought me immense joy and a sense of accomplishment and unveiled facets of myself that I never knew existed. As teachers, it is essential for us to continuously explore new things, not just for our teaching endeavors but also for our personal growth. Engaging in mental health breaks, such as hobbies, vacations, and yoga, can be transformative, unlocking hidden talents and insights we might have never imagined we possessed.

Delving into new activities allows us to tap into our curiosity and playfulness. These traits are often overshadowed by the responsibilities and challenges of our teaching profession. Taking these breaks from the routine nurtures our mental well-being, fostering a positive self-perception and overall equilibrium. Just like how we encourage our students to explore and discover, we should embrace this philosophy and create space for exploration in our own lives.

Taking up a new hobby or going on vacation leads to profound personal growth as we venture into uncharted territories and open ourselves to new experiences. As we dedicate time to activities that bring us joy and fulfillment, we nurture our mental health and promote resilience in the face of challenges. The insights we gain from these endeavors positively influence our teaching approach and classroom dynamics as we bring a renewed sense of enthusiasm and creativity into our lessons.

Furthermore, engaging in hobbies and leisure activities allows us to de-stress, recharge, and develop a healthy work-life balance. Our students benefit from having a knowledgeable, fulfilled, compassionate, and motivated teacher to make a difference in their lives.

## Mental Health Break

| Questions | Sample Answer | Your Answer |
| --- | --- | --- |
| **How can incorporating leisure activities improve your mental and emotional well-being?** | Engaging in hobbies provides a break from daily stressors and promotes relaxation. | |
| **What leisure activity will you set aside 30 minutes for this week, and how do you expect it to impact your mood?** | I, for instance, plan to read a book for 30 minutes and believe that I will feel relaxed. | |
| **How do enjoyable leisure activities influence your stress levels and emotional state?** | Participating in leisure activities such as listening to music can significantly reduce stress and improve well-being. | |

| | | |
|---|---|---|
| Identify three leisure activities that reduce stress for you. How will you intentionally engage in one of them each week? | Hiking, cooking, reading a book. For example, this week, I have planned to cook at least two homemade meals. | |
| Plan a mini-vacation or staycation for a long weekend. How will you use this time to unwind and recharge? | I'll have a picnic in the park then I'l read a book to disconnect from my work obligations. this will give me an opportunity to recharge. | |
| How do leisure activities act as "breathers" from work-related stressors, promoting joy and relaxation? | Watching a short TV episode (like a 30-minute sitcom episode) is a fundamental break in my workday that promotes relaxation. | |
| Set a timer for 10 minutes for a "breather" break during workdays. What enjoyable activity will you engage in during this time? | If it's just a 10-minute break, I might watch a funny video on YouTube. | |
| What advantage does a variety of activities have over a singular activity repeated? | When mentioning a variety of leisure activities these have to be from physical to creative activities and all of them improve my well-being in different ways. | |
| Create a list of different leisure activities and schedule one from each category. How will this contribute to a well-rounded sense of welfare? | Going out with friends promotes socialization, yoga promotes my physical being, and painting promotes my creativity. | |
| Meditate on your current self-care practices. How can a formalized self-care plan help you make consistent and intentional well-being choices? | A self-care plan helps with the prioritization of activities that are good for me. | |

| | | |
|---|---|---|
| **Develop a self-care plan with three activities. How will you incorporate them into your weekly routine?** | A nature walk, meditation, and reading;I try to do one of those a day during my workweek. | |
| **Set aside 15 minutes each morning for mindfulness. How will this practice clarify your thoughts and emotions, setting a positive intention for the day?** | Morning mindfulness provides a calm start of the day and helps identify my priorities for the day. | |
| **How does prioritizing self-care contribute to personal fulfillment and success, benefiting not only yourself but others, including your students?** | It ensures I'm mentally and emotionally ready to provide guidance to my students. | |
| **Invest in professional development aligned with your career goals. How does this investment enhance skills and demonstrate dedication to growth?** | For example, enrolling in online courses on educational technology enhances my skills which in turn helps me in my teaching and in my professional growth. | |
| **How can embracing curiosity and adventure enhance personal growth and well-being?** | Trying new activities promotes a sense of joy and discovery, which contributes to my personal growth. | |
| **How can mental health breaks create space for self-discovery and personal growth?** | They provide moments of reflection which allow me to find new passions and learn a little bit more about myself. | |
| **Keep a journal during your next mental health break. How will you record thoughts, feelings, and any new passions or insights that emerge?** | By documenting my experiences, and writing down any new interests that I might realize during those breaks. | |

| | | |
|---|---|---|
| **Reflect on the significance of continuous learning in your teaching profession. How does adopting a growth mindset benefit both you and your students?** | Continuous learning enhances teaching and instills a love for learning in students. for me it helps me grow professionally. | |
| **Commit to reading one education-related book or attending a professional development event. How will you apply the knowledge gained to enhance your teaching practices?** | For instance, if I read about innovative teaching methods, I'll be able to incorporate new strategies into my lessons so I can better engage my students. | |

# 7-Day Care Routine

| Day and time | Sample Activities/Food/Exercise for Body and Mind | Create Your Own |
|---|---|---|
| **Monday, 8:00 AM** | Begin the day with a 15-minute brisk walk for physical activity.<br><br>Breakfast: Enjoy a nutritious meal with scrambled eggs, spinach, and whole-grain toast.<br><br>Review and prioritize the day's lesson plans and tasks. | |
| **Monday, 8:45 AM** | Start the first teaching session with a focused approach.<br><br>Utilize the Pomodoro technique (25 minutes of teaching, followed by a 5-minute break).<br><br>Practice mindfulness techniques: Deep belly breathing and grounding exercises.<br><br>Stretching activity: Neck rolls and shoulder stretches. | |

| | |
|---|---|
| **Monday, 12:00 PM** | Take a lunch break; avoid eating in the classroom.<br><br>**Lunch:** Savor a chicken quinoa salad with mixed greens and a side of avocado.<br><br>**Mindfulness technique:** Mindful eating with attention to flavors and textures.<br><br>**Stretching activity:** Wrist and forearm stretches. |
| **Monday, 1:00 PM** | Resume teaching.<br><br>Incorporate yoga stretches: Downward dog and child's pose during short breaks. |
| **Monday, 4:00 PM** | Finish the teaching day with a final Pomodoro session.<br><br>Review the day's lessons and plan for the following day.<br><br>Take a brief walk to clear your mind and reflect on the day. |
| **Tuesday, 8:00 AM** | Begin the day with a 15-minute brisk walk for physical activity.<br><br>Breakfast: Enjoy a Greek yogurt parfait with fresh berries and a drizzle of honey.<br><br>Review your teaching schedule and prioritize tasks. |
| **Tuesday, 9:30 AM** | Attend a professional development class , online course or check out some of the suggested websites to enhance your skills. |

| | | |
|---|---|---|
| **Tuesday, 12:00 PM** | Take a lunch break focusing on a nutritious meal.<br><br>Lunch: Relish a salmon and quinoa bowl with steamed broccoli and a lemon vinaigrette.<br><br>Mindfulness technique: Guided body scan meditation.<br><br>Stretching activity: Hip flexor and quad stretches. | |
| **Tuesday, 1:00 PM** | Continue teaching.<br><br>Include quick exercises: Standing leg lifts and seated spinal twists during breaks. | |
| **Tuesday, 4:00 PM** | Finish the teaching day with a final Pomodoro session.<br><br>Reflect on your teaching accomplishments and plan for future lessons.<br><br>Spend quality time with your family or engage in a full-body stretching routine. | |
| **Wednesday, 8:00 AM** | Begin the day with a 15-minute brisk walk for physical activity.<br><br>Breakfast: Fuel up with oatmeal topped with sliced bananas and a sprinkle of chia seeds.<br><br>Review your teaching schedule and prioritize tasks. | |
| **Wednesday, 9:00 AM** | Participate in networking events or connect with fellow educators. | |

| | | |
|---|---|---|
| **Wednesday, 12:00 PM** | Take a lunch break with a balanced meal and stay hydrated.<br><br>Lunch: Enjoy a turkey and avocado wrap with a side of mixed greens.<br><br>Mindfulness technique: 5-4-3-2-1 grounding exercise.<br><br>Stretching activity: Spine and shoulder stretches. | |
| **Wednesday, 1:00 PM** | Return to teaching and incorporate quick exercises like lunges or seated calf raises between classes. | |
| **Wednesday, 4:00 PM** | Finish the teaching day with a final Pomodoro session.<br><br>Reflect on your teaching accomplishments and prepare a well-balanced dinner with grilled chicken and roasted vegetables.<br><br>Perform gentle neck and back stretches to unwind. | |
| **Thursday, 8:00 AM** | Begin the day with a 15-minute brisk walk for physical activity.<br><br>Breakfast: Indulge in a smoothie with kale, banana, and almond milk.<br><br>Review your teaching schedule and prioritize tasks. | |
| **Thursday, 8:45 AM** | Participate in mindfulness-based stress reduction with a focus on deep breathing and body scan. | |
| **Thursday, 12:00 PM** | Take a lunch break with a focus on mindful eating and relaxation.<br><br>Lunch: Enjoy a quinoa and chickpea salad with a lemon tahini dressing.<br><br>Stretching activity: Wrist and hand stretches. | |

| | | |
|---|---|---|
| **Thursday, 1:00 PM** | Return to teaching.<br><br>Take breaks for stretching to improve your posture and relieve any discomfort. | |
| **Thursday, 4:00 PM** | Finish the teaching day with a final Pomodoro session.<br><br>Reflect on your teaching accomplishments and engage in a mindfulness meditation session before dinner.<br><br>Include full-body stretches in your evening routine. | |
| **Friday, 8:00 AM** | Begin the day with a 15-minute brisk walk for physical activity.<br><br>Breakfast: Start the day with whole-grain pancakes topped with fresh berries. | |
| **Friday, 9:00 AM** | Review the week's teaching accomplishments and areas for improvement. | |
| **Friday, 12:00 PM** | Take a lunch break with a variety of vegetables and whole foods.<br><br>Lunch: Enjoy a Mediterranean quinoa bowl with hummus and olives.<br><br>Plan a self-care activity for the weekend to recharge.<br><br>Stretching activity: Ankle and calf stretches. | |
| **Friday, 1:00 PM** | Dedicate time to complete teaching tasks, grading and allocate time for continuous learning. | |

| | |
|---|---|
| **Friday, 4:00 PM** | Finish the teaching day with a final Pomodoro session. |
| | Review the day's teaching activities and send any necessary follow-up emails. |
| | End the week with a full-body stretching routine to unwind. |
| **Saturday and Sunday** | Here are some examples of how you can spend time outdoors, practice meditation, and engage in stretching and yoga exercises: |
| | Ways to Spend Time Outdoors: |
| | Nature Walks: Take leisurely walks in parks, nature reserves, or botanical gardens to connect with nature. |
| | Hiking: Explore nearby hiking trails to get some exercise while enjoying the beauty of the outdoors. |
| | Picnics: Plan a picnic with your family or colleagues and savor a meal in the open air. |
| | Outdoor Yoga: Practice yoga in a serene outdoor setting, like a park or beach, to enhance your practice. |
| | Gardening: Cultivate a small garden at home or participate in a community garden project to nurture plants and enjoy fresh air. |
| | Cycling: Ride your bicycle around your neighborhood or on dedicated bike trails for physical activity and fresh air. |
| | Outdoor Games: Organize outdoor games like frisbee, badminton, or soccer with friends and family. |
| | Photography: Capture the beauty of nature with photography, whether it's birds, landscapes, or flowers. |

Meditation Techniques:

Mindfulness Meditation: Focus on your breath and observe your thoughts without judgment. This helps in reducing stress and increasing self-awareness.

Guided Meditation: Follow recorded meditation sessions led by experts to guide you through relaxation and visualization exercises.

Body Scan Meditation: Pay attention to each part of your body, starting from your toes to your head, releasing tension and promoting relaxation.

Loving-Kindness Meditation: Cultivate feelings of love and compassion by repeating positive affirmations for yourself and others.

Transcendental Meditation: Use a mantra to achieve a deep state of relaxation and heightened awareness.

Stretching Exercises:

Neck Stretches: Gently tilt your head from side to side, forward and backward to relieve neck tension.

Shoulder Rolls: Roll your shoulders forward and backward to loosen shoulder muscles.

Chest Opener: Clasp your hands behind your back and gently lift your chest to open up the front of your body.

Hamstring Stretch: Sit on the floor with one leg extended, bend the other knee, and reach for your toes on the extended leg.

Quad Stretch: Stand and pull one foot behind you, holding your ankle to stretch your quadriceps.

Calf Stretch: Stand with one foot in front of the other and lean forward to stretch the calf muscle.

Yoga Exercises:

**Child's** Pose: Kneel on the floor, sit **back on** your heels, and stretch your **arms** forward while resting your **forehead** on the ground.

**Downward** Dog: Start in a push-up **position,** lift your hips, and form an **inverted** "V" shape with your body.

**Warrior** Pose: Stand with your legs **apart,** extend your arms, and bend one **knee** while keeping the other leg **straight.**

**Cobra** Pose: Lie on your stomach, place **your palms** under your shoulders, and **lift your** upper body while keeping your **pelvis on** the ground.

**Tree Pose:** Stand on one leg, place the **sole of** the other foot against your inner **thigh,** and bring your hands to your **chest in** a prayer position.

**Cat-Cow** Stretch: Get on your hands **and knees,** arch your back upward **(cat), and** then lower it down (cow).

**Remember,** it's essential to choose **activities** that you enjoy and that suit **your** fitness level. Regular outdoor **time,** meditation, and stretching or **yoga can** help teachers manage stress, **enhance** physical health, and promote **overall** well-being.

**Toward a Happier, Healthier Teaching Community**

In the spirit of the community we form when we enter the teaching profession, I ask you now to help me reach more teachers so we can improve the quality of life across the board – both for our fellow teachers and for our students.

Simply by sharing your honest opinion of this book and a little about your own experience, you'll show other teachers where they can find the vital self-care advice they're looking for.

Thank you so much for your support. I wish you joy and fulfillment in every teaching day.

# CONCLUSION

As we reach the final pages of this book, let us take a moment to reflect on the core message woven through each chapter: your well-being is of utmost importance. Amidst the demands of teaching, we must always remember to care for ourselves, which is the key to becoming our best educators.

Throughout our journey together, we've explored the Le.AR.N. method—a simple yet powerful framework that empowers us to create a self-care routine that truly works for us—among other approaches. We've delved into the significance of setting boundaries, discovering our community, and embracing leisure activities to nurture our mental health and overall well-being. The power of self-compassion has been highlighted, as we've learned that investing in ourselves through self-care is not selfish; it's a testament to our commitment to personal fulfillment and success.

Teaching is rewarding but demanding, sometimes leading to stress and burnout. Nevertheless, with the insights from this book, you have the tools to overcome these challenges and rediscover the joy and passion that brought you to this noble profession in the first place. Maintain hope even if you find yourself in the initial stages of burnout. Start small and gradually build your self-care routine, incorporating activities that bring joy and moments of play and exploration.

As educators, we acknowledge the importance of lifelong learning. This journey is not just about imparting knowledge to others; it's also about continuously learning and growing ourselves. Embrace the thrill of discovery and keep exploring new hobbies, interests, and passions without end. This way, you enhance your teaching abilities and fuel your sense of self and overall well-being.

Before we bid farewell, I wish to extend my heartfelt appreciation to each of you for embarking on this journey toward self-care and well-being with me. Your commitment to your profession and your students is praiseworthy. This book has offered valuable insights and practical strategies to enrich your life as an educator.

If this book has resonated with you and helped you find new ways to care for yourself, I would be grateful if you could take a moment to leave a review on Amazon. Your words may inspire other teachers to embark on their own journey to self-care, positively impacting the teaching community.

As we navigate the ever-changing education landscape, remember you are not alone. We are a community of teachers, learners, and seekers of knowledge, and together, we can uplift and support one another on this rewarding path.

Wishing you a life filled with joy, purpose, and abundant self-care.

# REFERENCES


Algorani, E.B & Gupta, V. (2021). Coping mechanisms. National Library of Medicine. National Center for Biotechnology Information. In StatPearls. https://www.ncbi.nlm.nih.gov/books/NBK559031/

Alhola, P., & Polo-Kantola, P. (2007). Sleep deprivation: Impact on cognitive performance. Neuropsychiatric Disease and Treatment, 3(5), 553–567. doi 10.2147/NDT.S797

Brandy. (2023, January 25). *Self care quotes for teachers*. The Counseling Teacher. https://thecounselingteacher.com/2018/07/self-care-quotes-for-teachers.html

Brainy Quote. (2000). Walt Disney quote. https://www.brainyquote.com/quotes/walt_disney_132637

Cleveland Clinic. (n.d.). Stress. https://my.clevelandclinic.org/health/articles/11874-stress

Ellevate Network. (2017, September 12). Quotes about the power of community. https://www.ellevatenetwork.com/articles/8538-quotes-about-the-power-of-community

Folta, S. C., Lichtenstein, A. H., Seguin, R. A., Goldberg, J. P., Corbin, M. A., Wiker, N., ... & Economos, C. D. (2020). Teachers' nutrition-related classroom practices in the context of childhood obesity prevention: A pilot study. Nutrients, 12(5), 1308. doi:10.3390/nu12051308

Gardner, B. (2015). A review and analysis of the use of 'habit' in understanding, predicting, and influencing health-related behavior. Health Psychology Review, 9(3), 277–295. doi: 10.1080/17437199.2013.876238

Ghonge, M. M., Bag, R., & Singh, A. (2020). Indian education: Ancient, medieval, and modern. In www.intechopen.com. IntechOpen. https://www.intechopen.com/chapters/73290

Hillman, C. H., Erickson, K. I., & Kramer, A. F. (2008). Be smart, exercise your heart: Exercise effects on brain and cognition. Nature Reviews Neuroscience, 9(1), 58-65. doi 10.1038/nrn2298

Hollenbeck, J. R., Klein, H. J., O'Leary, A. M., & Wright, P. M. (1989). Investigation of the construct validity of a self-report measure of goal commitment. Journal of Applied Psychology, 74(6), 951-956. doi:10.1037/0021-9010.74.6.951

Jagoo, K. (2021, July 19). Taking breaks is key to learning, research shows. Verywell Mind. https://www.verywellmind.com/why-research-shows-that-taking-breaks-is-key-to-learning-5190398

Katon, W., Lin, E. H. B., & Kroenke, K. (2007). The association of depression and anxiety with medical symptom burden in patients with chronic medical illness. General Hospital Psychiatry, 29(2), 147–155. https://doi.org/10.1016/j.genhosppsych.2006.11.005

Kim, E. S., Shiba, K., Boehm, J. K., & Kubzansky, L. D. (2020). A sense of purpose in life and five health behaviors in older adults. Preventive Medicine, 139, 106172. https://doi.org/10.1016/j.ypmed.2020.106172

Latham, G. P., & Locke, E. A. (2007). New Developments in and Directions for Goal-Setting Research. European Psychologist, 12(4), 290-300. doi:10.1027/1016-9040.12.4.290

Lazarus, R. S., & Folkman, S. (1984). Stress, appraisal, and coping. Springer Publishing Company.

Locke, E. A., & Latham, G. P. (2006). New directions in goal-setting theory. Current Directions in Psychological Science, 15(5), 265-268. doi:10.1111/j.1467-8721.2006.00449.x

Loprinzi, P. D., Frith, E., Edwards, M. K., Sng, E., Ashpole, N. (2020). The effects of exercise on memory function among young to middle-aged adults: Systematic review and recommendations for future research. American Journal of Health Promotion, 34(8), 874–887. doi 10.1177/0890117120924666

McLoughlin, D. (2023, May 16). Teacher burnout statistics. WordsRated – The data of books. https://wordsrated.com/teacher-burnout-statistics/

Morin, A. (n.d.). Brain breaks: What you need to know. Understood.https://www.understood.org/en/articles/evidence-based-behavior-strategy-brain-breaks

Parker, E. A., Feinberg, T. M., Lane, H. G., Deitch, R., Zemanick, A., Saksvig, B. I., Turner, L., & Hager, E. R. (2020). The diet quality of elementary and middle school teachers is associated with healthier nutrition-related classroom practices. Preventive Medicine Reports, 18, 101087. https://doi.org/10.1016/j.pmedr.2020.101087

Perera, R. (2023, January 17). How (and why) to use the 52/17 rule to boost productivity. Freelancing Hacks. https://www.freelancinghacks.com/how-why-use-the-5217-rule-for-productivity/

Pressman, S. D., Matthews, K. A., Cohen, S., Martire, L. M., Scheier, M., Baum, A., & Schulz, R. (2009). Association of enjoyable leisure activities with psychological and physical well-being. Psychosomatic Medicine, 71(7), 725–732. https://doi.org/10.1097/psy.0b013e3181ad7978

Rekhi, S. (n.d.). Coping mechanisms. Berkeley Well-being. https://www.berkeleywellbeing.com/coping-mechanisms.html

Robbins, R. (2020, April 22). Why asking for help is so hard, and how to get better at it. CNBC. https://www.cnbc.com/2020/04/22/why-asking-for-help-is-so-hard-and-how-to-get-better-at-it.html

Science of Happiness Podcast. (2023, July 13). Purpose. Greater Good. https://greatergood.berkeley.edu/topic/purpose

Scroggs, L. (n.d.). The Pomodoro Technique: A complete guide to time management. Todoist. https://todoist.com/productivity-methods/pomodoro-technique

Simkin, J. (2020, January.). Education in the Middle Ages. Spartacus Educational. https://spartacus-educational.com/YALDeducation.htm#:~:text=It%20was%20usually%20only%20the

Steiner, E. D., Tabler, J., Simon, M., & Baird, M. D. (2022). Educator well-being in the United States: Findings from the American Educator Panels 2022 Educator Well-being Survey. RAND Corporation. https://www.rand.org/pubs/research_reports/RRA1011-2.html

Suni, S & Singh, A. (2023, July). How much sleep do we really need? Sleep Foundation. https://www.sleepfoundation.org/how-sleep-works/how-much-sleep-do-we-really-need

U.S. Department of Education. (n.d.). Teaching. https://www.ed.gov/teaching

U.S. Department of Health and Human Services (HHS). (2018). Physical activity guidelines for Americans. https://health.gov/our-work/physical-activity/current-guidelines

Wooll, M. (2021, November 3). The importance of community. BetterUp. https://www.betterup.com/blog/importance-of-community

Yaribeygi, H., Panahi, Y., Sahraei, H., Johnston, T. P., & Sahebkar, A. (2017). The impact of stress on body function: A review. EXCLI Journal, 16(1), 1057–1072. https://doi.org/10.17179/excli2017-480